THE MAKING OF PSYCHOHISTORY

The Making of Psychohistory is the first volume dedicated to the history of psychohistory, an amalgam of psychology, history, and related social sciences. Dr. Paul Elovitz, a participant since the early days of the organized field, recounts the origins and development of this interdisciplinary area of study, as well as the contributions of influential individuals working within the intersection of historical and psychological thinking and methodologies. This is an essential, thorough reflection on the rich and varied scholarship within psychohistory's subfields of applied psychoanalysis, political psychology, and psychobiography.

Paul H. Elovitz, PhD, is a founding member and past president of the International Psychohistorical Association, founder of the Psychohistory Forum, founder and editor-in-chief of the journal *Clio's Psyche*, and a founding member of Ramapo College of New Jersey where he teaches history, interdisciplinary studies, and psychohistory. He practiced psychotherapy for a quarter century after extensive training in psychoanalysis, and is the author of over 340 publications.

THE MAKING OF PSYCHOHISTORY

Origins, Controversies, and Pioneering Contributors

Paul H. Elovitz

Routledge
Taylor & Francis Group

NEW YORK AND LONDON

First published 2018
by Routledge
711 Third Avenue, New York, NY 10017

and by Routledge
2 Park Square, Milton Park, Abingdon, Oxon, OX14 4RN

Routledge is an imprint of the Taylor & Francis Group, an informa business

Library of Congress Cataloging-in-Publication Data
Names: Elovitz, Paul H., author.
Title: The making of psychohistory : origins, controversies, and
    pioneering contributors / Paul H. Elovitz.
Description: New York, NY : Routledge, 2018. | Includes
    bibliographical references and index.
Identifiers: LCCN 2018001658 (print) | LCCN 2018002817 (ebook) |
    ISBN 9780429503917 (eBook) | ISBN 9781138587489 (hardback) |
    ISBN 9781138587496 (pbk.)
Subjects: LCSH: Psychohistory—History.
Classification: LCC D16.16 (ebook) | LCC D16.16 .E46 2018 (print) |
    DDC 901/.9—dc23
LC record available at https://lccn.loc.gov/2018001658

ISBN: 978-1-138-58748-9 (hbk)
ISBN: 978-1-138-58749-6 (pbk)
ISBN: 978-0-429-50391-7 (ebk)

Typeset in Bembo
by Apex CoVantage, LLC

To my wife, Geri, children David, Laura, and Marc, and all my psychohistorical colleagues

CONTENTS

PSYCHOHISTORY

What happened *why* is the historian's
Agenda. *What* potentially extends
To every action of the common man's,
So that the controversy never ends
Concerning which bits of the human past
To privilege. The stakes are high because
The *what* can shape the why. Why empires last,
Or birth rates fall, or tools emerge, or laws,
Are loaded questions that construe the *what*
As empires, birth rates, tools, or laws—that float
These as the active entities and not
The people doing what those terms denote.
All *what*s come down to human doings. See:
All *why*s thus end in psychohistory.

Rudolph Binion
Written for the annual compendium
of *Clio's Psyche*

ACKNOWLEDGMENTS

There are so many individuals to thank that it's difficult to know where to begin. My friends David Beisel, Ken Fuchsman, and Peter Petschauer are three of the individuals who have made this book possible. Beisel always inspired me with his brilliant insights and ability to teach psychohistory with great clarity and depth of understanding. He also helped me with my writing despite my insecurities about it, until I realized that I was placing too much of a burden on him. I simultaneously became angered by one of his critiques of what I erroneously thought was my best work possible. In anger I then very clearly said to him that our friendship was much more important than any help he could give me with my writing, and since then I have only troubled him to verify some issues of fact or refresh my memory. David has always encouraged my work of documenting and analyzing the history of psychohistory.

Ken Fuchsman is a friend who is quick to show his appreciation to me and to others after coming to the organized field of psychohistory rather late in his career. In most of my quarter century process of collecting the materials for and talking about writing *The Making of Psychohistory*, he saw the divergence between my intention to work on the book and becoming distracted by teaching, editing, presidential elections, running the Psychohistory Forum, and other projects. Ken continuously encouraged me to write articles that would in fact be part of my book project, or at least got me thinking along the same lines. He then read the draft book in its entirety and shared his detailed knowledge of Freud and the early Freud circle. As my project has reached fruition, I wish him success with his most ambitious book, *The Nature of Being Human*. My friends and colleagues Peter Petschauer and Howard Stein showed a willingness to be sounding boards for me in writing this book as I fought distractions from so many other activities. Unfortunately, the 2016 presidential election and teaching stood in the way of my utilizing their help effectively. Petschauer inspired me as he devoted much of his retirement from teaching to writing a series of books. Generously, he read and carefully responded to several drafts of my book and shared his knowledge of psychohistory in Europe. Jim Anderson, David Beisel, John Hartman, Joyce Rosenberg, and Neil Wilson all read the entire manuscript and made comments. For reading specific parts of the volume and commenting my thanks to Deb Hayden and Mac Runyan.

It is the youngest member of the Psychohistory Forum for whom I presently feel great appreciation. David Cifelli came to my freshman class as a seventeen-year-old honors student, and before the year was out, I was working with him as a mentor as well as a co-author and younger colleague. He wrote or co-authored six articles with me or another colleague. I kept talking about making progress on my book and Cifelli not only listened, but also helped me get back on track to achieving my goal. Thanks to Dean Stephen Rice, two small Ramapo College Student/Faculty research grants fortunately helped David's finances, but money was never his main objective. Rather, he seemed motivated by the search for knowledge and friendship and the desire to work closely with a mentor. Without relinquishing his plan of leaving Ramapo after three years to attend Rutgers School of Dental Medicine in pursuit of his professional goal, he has expressed an appreciation and a talent for psychohistory that is unusual in a twenty-year-old. My wife and I have offered to adopt David, despite his having wonderful parents. I also want to thank Ramapo College for providing a one-semester sabbatical early in this century to help me make progress on this book. Regrettably, most of this release time was also absorbed by my writing psychobiographies for a presidential election.

For valuable information in researching this book I would like to thank James W. Anderson, Robert Begtrup, David Beisel, Marilyn Charles, Nick Duffell, Karl Figlio, Larry Friedman, Ken Fuchsman, John Hartman, Deborah Hayden, Susan Hein, Juhani Ihanus, Peter Lawner, Bob Lentz, Peter Loewenberg, David Lotto, Richard Lyman, William Meyers, Martin Quitt, Peter Redman, William McKinley Runyan, Ludmila Shimelevich, Howard Stein, Christina Stern, Charles Strozier, Frank J. Sulloway, Jacques Szaluta, and so many others. Thanks also to Larry Friedman for advising me on publishers and Ken Fuchsman who is mentoring me on how to help more colleagues learn about the publication of *The Making of Psychohistory*.

There are so many individuals to be thanked within the psychohistory movement and elsewhere. There are colleagues who have mentored me along the way, including the late Sid Halpern, Mel Goldstein, and Monte Ullman. My psychoanalyst, Neil Wilson, deserves special thanks for helping me grow, as does my wife, Geri. Through the years I have worked on this book, I have had some very capable and devoted young people who have aided me in this process amidst mostly working on other projects with me. Caitlin Adams Gaynor used her excellent editorial skills a few days before she gave birth to her second child and not very long thereafter. Nicole D'Andria was always available on short notice to check for errors, edit, and otherwise be helpful. Pictures of many psychohistorical pioneers were excluded from this book due to concerns regarding image quality and permissions. Fortunately, these are available at our website (cliospsyche. org) along with many other valuable materials on the history and teaching of psychohistory. In earlier periods Devin McGinley, Nicole Alliegro, Brett Lobatto, Gary Schmidt, and Vicki Walsh helped as I gathered materials and did some preliminary work on the subject. Nicole and I worked together to create the index which Bob Lentz painstakingly corrected and refined. The Ramapo College graphic artist Jose Hernandez created the image on the paperback cover of a face looking outward and inward simultaneously. I also want to express my appreciation to the helpful librarians of Franklin Lakes and Ramapo College, as well as to all of my colleagues in the Psychohistory Forum, the International Psychohistorical Association, and in the entire psychohistorical community. Finally, Lillian Rand, Jamie Magyar, Sheri Sipka, Kristina Siosyte, and others on the Routledge team deserve credit for their cooperativeness and efficiency in getting my book to the reader in a timely fashion.

GLOSSARY

American Historical Association   **AHA**

American Historical Review   **AHR**

Association for the Psychoanalysis of Culture and Society (1994–)   **APCS**

*Clio's Psyche: The "Why" of Culture, Society, History, and
Current Events* (1994–)   *Clio*

Group for the Use of Psychology in History (1972–1999)   **GUPH**

The History of Childhood Quarterly: The Journal of Psychohistory
(1973–1978)   **Journal**

International Dialogue Initiative (2008–)   **IDI (Volkan)**

Institute for Psychohistory (1975–)   **Institute**

The Journal of Psychohistory (1973–)   **Journal**

International Psychohistorical Association (1978–)   **IPA**

International Society for Political Psychology (1978–)   **ISPP**

New York University   **NYU**

Psychohistory News: Newsletter of the International Psychohistorical Association
(1978–)   **Psychohistory News**

Psychohistory Forum (1982–)   **Forum**

Psychohistory Review (1972–1999)   **Review**

Group for the Study of Psychohistorical Process
(Lifton, 1966–2015)   **Wellfleet**

SOME OFTEN MENTIONED CONTRIBUTORS

David Beisel (1938–)
Rudolph Binion (1927–2011)
Lloyd deMause (1931–)
Erik Erikson (1902–1994)
Sigmund Freud (1856–1939)
Lawrence J. Friedman (1940–)
Peter Gay (1923–2015)
Sidney Halpern (1927–1994)
Henry Lawton (1941–2014)
Robert Jay Lifton (1926–)
Peter Loewenberg (1933–)
Howard Stein (1946–)
Peter Petschauer (1939–)
Charles B. Strozier (1940–)
Montague Ullman (1916–2008)
Vamık Volkan (1932–)

1

INTRODUCTION

Although the organized field of psychohistory is a half century old, there is still no comprehensive history of it,[1] to say nothing of the century of studies from the Freud circle on. As an Eriksonian participant-observer and scholar of this valuable movement delving into human motivation, I think it is incumbent on me to commit my experiences and knowledge to print before they are lost to time. This is a personal memoir of my experiences in the field since the late 1960s, as well as its history. I have been a "big tent" psychohistorian, open to all perspectives and welcoming all colleagues to meetings I have organized since 1976 and to the pages of *Clio's Psyche*, the journal I edit.

Thoughtful people do psychohistory whether or not they realize it. Psychological assumptions underlie any assessment—or even comment about—history, human interaction, and society. We humans want to know why things happen. The psychological assumptions underlying these speculations are seldom well thought out or developed. Thus, all historians do a type of psychohistory without realizing it. Regrettably, academic historians as a group reject the field of psychohistory for a variety of reasons, including their suspicion of the new, dislike of psychoanalysis, uneasiness with the unconscious and irrational forces in others and themselves, and fear that their knowledge of human motivation will be exposed as inadequate. Highly speculative and poorly researched and thought-out psychobiographies have also hurt the reputation of our field. Applying a psychiatric diagnosis to a historical personality or president is sometimes passed off as psychohistory rather than dismissed as speculation or a starting point for serious research. Working with the unconscious is difficult, and researching childhood and personality materials involves lots of hard work. As an author, editor, and organizer of meetings, my ideal has been to set a high standard for research, and avoid psychopathologizing the subject and even technical terminology. I have always rejected reductionism as anathema to good psychological scholarship. Psychoanalysts sometimes dismiss psychohistorical studies of historical personages on the grounds that there is not a living patient to get information from and to confirm or disprove the psychohistorian's assessment. Our subjects may not usually be alive, but their biographers are breathing human beings who both need to understand the countertransference they bring to their subjects and to deepen and broaden their understanding of unconscious processes and the complexities of human beings. Despite these resistances and difficulties, our field has developed an enormous literature and various methodologies, making for a level of professional competence and expertise not available to those who rely on their own amateur, unnamed psychohistorical assumptions.

Psychohistory has opened new realms of understanding. The integration of psychoanalysis, and psychology generally, with the humanities and social sciences has enormously increased our knowledge of people's lives. In history graduate schools, professors were inclined to explain motivation by vague, amorphous references to economic, political, and social forces, whereas psychohistory provided insights into specific real life human complexities, emotions, motivations, personalities, and traumas. Psychohistory opened doors of understanding of behaviors that had been previously written off as meaningless. Patterns became discernable. Psychohistory provides a depth of understanding of the human propensity to have enemies and sometimes go to war against them not found elsewhere. Biographies written before Freud, psychobiography, and psychohistory were so much less revealing than those written today, which look into the minds of the characters. Innovative colleagues from numerous disciplines have created a major interdisciplinary accomplishment, which is usually labeled as psychohistory, political psychology, and applied psychoanalysis. I define psychohistory as an amalgam of psychology, history, and related social sciences. It focuses on the "why" of history, especially the difference between intention and actual behavior. Psychobiography, childhood, group dynamics, mechanisms of psychic defense, reactions to trauma, unconscious motivation, dreams, and creativity are primary areas of research. There are other, related definitions of psychohistory by distinguished colleagues.[2]

The language of psychology has come to permeate modern consciousness, as indicated by the everyday use of terms such as anxiety, denial, ego, empathy, guilt, id, identity, masochist, narcissism, neurotic, obsessive-compulsive, paranoid, posttraumatic stress disorder (PTSD), sadism, split personality, subconscious, superego, and unconscious. Laypeople read or hear about therapy and try to raise their children based in part on what some television psychologist has said. Given the ubiquity of psychological language, the concept of applying psychology to history and society becomes commonsensical. Thus, when the average person first hears the words "psycho" and "history" linked together, the question is: What is it? Then, the usual answer is: "Oh, that makes perfect sense. What a good idea!"

The spread of psychological knowledge can be illustrated by Richard H. Thaler earning a 1917 Nobel Prize in Economics for applying psychology to

"economic decision-making." *Clio's Psyche* has published articles on psychoeconomics, including a 2009 special issue on the subject. The rational man model of
human behavior is increasingly being supplanted by a more sophisticated understanding of human motivation based on the pioneering work of psychoanalysts,
psychohistorians, and behavioral scientists. Psychological approaches to knowledge in many disciplines are currently being stimulated by continuing discoveries
in neuroscience, which validate much of the theoretical work of Freud and others.
The endeavors of Nobel Prize-winning neuroscientist Eric Kandel are a good
illustration of this. Naturally, it takes time for practitioners in the field to catch up
with the latest cutting edge work.

As of this moment, despite many struggles, psychohistory may not have gained
respectability in all but a few history and psychology departments at major universities, but in other departments and medical schools there have been a fair
number of contributors. Today, clinicians of various backgrounds, and especially
psychoanalysts, form the largest group attending the meetings of the International Psychohistorical Association (IPA), the Association for the Psychoanalysis
of Culture and Society (APCS), and the Psychohistory Forum. Whatever their
background or location, those doing psychohistory and political psychology have
provided invaluable insights and methodologies for biographers, scholars generally, and the general public to use. Serious biographers use our insights, sometimes
denouncing Freud and psychohistory in the process. Thus they have their cake
and eat it too. As the Pulitzer Prize-winning best-selling historian Barbara Tuchman wrote in 1975, "All good history is psychohistory."[3] Colleagues who read this
volume will see how it showcases the work of the pioneers of psychohistory and
my half-century in fostering the field as a midwife of psychohistorical knowledge
and a scholar in my own right.

My role is as an advocate, creator, editor, historian, organizer, and researcher of
psychohistory. I discovered psychoanalysis and psychohistory in the 1960s while
teaching at Temple University in Philadelphia and immediately read all of the
studies I could find. In 1971 I became a founding faculty member of Ramapo
College, a well-respected public liberal arts institution in northern New Jersey,
and I started teaching psychohistory. I became affiliated with the Institute for
Psychohistory in 1975, where the following year I co-founded and ran its Saturday Workshop Seminars. In that year I also attended the first national psychohistorical conference and the International Psychohistorical Association, of which
I became an officer and would go on to hold most offices, including its presidency.
In 1982 I founded the Psychohistory Forum, which holds Saturday Seminars in
Manhattan and at international conferences. As an organizer of meetings, I have
always been open to all different approaches to psychohistory. My editorial service has been on *The Journal of Psychohistory* and as founder and editor-in-chief
of *Clio's Psyche*, which I created in 1994. *Clio* has had a double-blind refereeing
system for more than two decades, an aspect of the journal of which I'm very
proud. In 1976 I began my career as a presidential political psychologist and

psychobiographer; I have made presentations on every president since Ford, and I have written forty-three related articles and chapters of books, including three on Donald J. Trump. The largest number of my hundreds of other publications have been on the contributions and lives of my colleagues, dreams, historical methodology, psychobiography, and teaching psychohistory.[4] For over two decades I have been specifically researching this book, which is structured as follows.

The organization of *The Making of Psychohistory* is partly chronological and mostly topical. Professor Rudolph Binion's poem "Psychohistory" was written initially for the compendium of the best articles in *Clio's Psyche*—it does a good job succinctly explaining in 100 words what psychohistory is about. In this introduction, my goal is to explain the purpose of this volume and to give you a sense of who psychohistorians are and what we do. Below I will explain it chapter by chapter.

"My Exuberant Journey" represents my introduction to psychoanalysis and psychohistory so the reader can understand how and why I fell in love with psychological history that I had not been taught while earning a doctoral degree in modern European history. I move on to "The Early History of Psychohistory" to help the reader understand that this method of understanding did not begin with the creation of organized groups beginning in 1966 and blossoming in the 1970s, but rather has a history that extends for more than a century. In "Resistance and Perseverance," I spell out the decision made by academic history and psychology departments to reject a method of inquiry that was capturing the imagination of so many young and some not so young scholars, and then go on to point out the perseverance of determined and talented colleagues in creating a vast literature.

Next, in "Comparing the Early Freudian and Psychohistorical Movements," I describe and explain the early psychohistory done in the Freud circle and in the more than fifty years before the creation of specific psychohistorical and psychological institutions. There is considerable comparison in this chapter of the two leaders who started organizations with the initials IPA: Sigmund Freud and Lloyd deMause. The founder of *The Journal of Psychohistory* is included not because he is the best known and respected of the modern proponents of psychohistory, but because he is its most vocal advocate and institution builder, and the person I know best.

Our lives start in childhood and perhaps the most important thing that psychohistory did for historians was to emphasize the importance of early experiences. Consequently, I move on to "A Psychohistorian's Approach to Childhood and Childrearing." In choosing outstanding contributors to the field, I have focused on colleagues who have been specific advocates of psychohistory, even though one of them preferred the term "psychological history." Consequently, my next two chapters are on Lifton, deMause, Volkan, Gay, Loewenberg, and Binion, all of whom I've had the opportunity to meet and work with.[5]

As a college professor I love teaching and my students, which explains the placement of the next chapter, "My Journey as a Psychohistorical Teacher."

Readers should note that throughout the book I have interspersed the personal with the professional as a way of both telling my story and of humanizing a field that would be a mistake to present abstractly. After all, the essence of psychohistory is that we have brought real, live, complex, flesh-and-blood persons center stage into the historical arena while professional historians have been inclined to focus on broad movements and factors. We dare to probe irrationality in individuals and groups rather than simply declaring certain individuals to be crazy and groups to be consumed by unruly emotion.

In "My Role in Creating and Nurturing Postgraduate Psychohistorical Education," I present my philosophy as a midwife of psychohistorical knowledge as an organizer and editor. Although I started graduate school in the Department of Political Science at Rutgers University, I never expected that I would become a student of the presidential candidates and presidents. That this happened is but one of the many extraordinary opportunities I've had as a psychohistorian working to understand my society and its leadership. This opportunity has created many predicaments, which I cover in "The Dilemmas of a Presidential Psychohistorian." There's no more powerful person in our contemporary world than the American president, which is one of the reasons I have devoted so much time and attention to the exhausting job of following our presidential aspirants and those who succeeded in the period from 1976 to the present.

In "Finding My Voice with Halpern, deMause, and Ullman," I spell out my struggles in being powerfully influenced by three strong individuals. To me, it would not be fair to the very numerous colleagues I've worked with if I didn't mention some of them, thus "Builders of Psychohistory." Finally, in "Concluding Thoughts," I provide some additional insights on the field and my motivations for performing the roles I have. Of course, I also summarized some of my main points. My hope is that these introductory comments will help the reader have an understanding of the organization of the volume.

Well over a hundred builders of psychohistory are discussed in this volume, with two chapters devoted specifically to six leaders of the field: Rudolph Binion, Lloyd deMause, Peter Gay, Robert Jay Lifton, Peter Loewenberg, and Vamık Volkan. This group of psychohistorians is comprised of three historians, two psychiatrists, and a leader of the organized field who dropped out of a doctoral program when he was not allowed to write an explicitly psychoanalytic and psychohistorical dissertation. All but one had at least some psychoanalytic training. They started psychohistorical organizations and together wrote over a hundred books that have done much to define the field. Robert Lifton is an unusual psychiatrist who studied groups, individuals, movements, and societies rather than treating patients. With others, he created the Group for the Study of Psychohistorical Process in 1966 and ran famous seminars in his Cape Cod summer home until 2015. In New York City, he created an important center of applied psychohistory focused on issues of violence and human survival in the nuclear age. While Lifton says psychohistory is a method of inquiry, Lloyd deMause devoted his life to creating an actual discipline of psychohistory. Toward this end, deMause created a psychohistorical institute, international association, and printing press, edited *The History of Child-hood* (1974), and wrote *The Foundations of Psychohistory* (1982). These conflicting visions have had an enormous influence on psychohistory. Vamık Volkan, the author of *The Need to Have Enemies and Allies: From Clinical Practice to International Relations* (1988) and *Enemies on the Couch* (2013), is a Cypriote-Turkish-American psychiatrist who created a psychohistorical center and journal devoted to lessening hatred and conflict in our world. All three of these men have a passion for creating a more peaceful world.

The remaining three leaders are historians who have done outstanding psychohistorical work. Peter Gay was an excellent scholar whose books provide enormous insights into European history and Sigmund Freud. Peter Loewenberg, who like Gay was a refugee from Nazi Germany, has been a leader of psychoanalysis and psychohistory and played a key role in bringing Western psychotherapy to China. Rudolph Binion was a brilliant historian who focused on traumatic reliving among individuals and societies after rejecting his early Freudianism. I interviewed four of these six psychohistorical leaders and arranged for and published interviews of the other two. After publishing memorials by twenty-three colleagues for my good friend Rudolph Binion, I was inspired to honor Lifton, Loewenberg, and Volkan with Festschriften because I much prefer to appreciate the living rather than the dead.[6]

Colleagues most familiar with psychohistory may wonder why I've chosen not to have Erik Homburger Erikson (1902–1994) listed in the title of a chapter, especially because I am a proponent of Erikson's disciplined subjectivity.[7] The answer is based on several factors. First, he is discussed at length elsewhere.[8] Although Erikson's *Young Man Luther* (1958) played a major role in drawing the attention of much of the academic community to the possibility of doing psychohistory, it was less original than is usually thought. The Reformation historian Preserved Smith, in 1913 (not 1915 as on page 28 of *Young Man Luther*), wrote a valuable psychoanalytic study of the founder of Lutheranism, which Erikson should have credited more than criticized. Furthermore, as a historian, Erikson was rather weak, and I'm inclined to think that Norman O. Brown did a better job on Luther in a single chapter of *Life Against Death* (1969) than Erikson did in the entire book. I am not a fan of his eight-stage theory of personality, which is too formulaic for my taste. Importantly, Erikson disliked the term psychohistory and opposed creating a separate field of psychohistory. He certainly played an important role in inspiring Robert Jay Lifton, including in discouraging the creation of a separate academic field, which I consider to be unfortunate.

It is not just leaders and the most prominent who create knowledge and an area of study. Many different colleagues contributed to our field and over sixty were interviewed in-depth in *Clio's Psyche*. I will describe the group I have worked with using statistics, then delve more deeply into our subject. At the start of this project, it was my hope to have a major statistical breakdown of the featured scholars and editors appearing in *Clio's Psyche*.[9] While I recognize that not all accomplished psychohistorians were interviewed as featured scholars in the period that begins in 1994 with the initiation of *Clio's Psyche*, the overwhelming majority was interviewed. This sample is thus suggestive rather than definitive.

The categories I sought to include are gender, geographical region, primary affiliation, religious background, self-identification, and training of the featured scholars. However, I've decided to settle for a much more limited statistical analysis, mostly because of the limited data and the need to see this project to completion, as well as my own qualitative, rather than quantitative, capabilities and inclinations. The featured scholars and editors interviewed by Bob Lentz, others, and me is the base that I'm using for this purpose with some exceptions.[10] In the end, the following statistics were calculated using a group of sixty-one featured scholars and editors.

Ninety percent of the psychohistorians live in the United States, including Sander Breiner, Peter Gay, Jay Gonen, George Kren, Peter Loewenberg, and Peter Petschauer, who were born abroad. The remaining ten percent of psychohistorians interviewed are in countries other than the United States: Canada, England, Germany, Italy, and the Netherlands. Canadian and Dutch scholars Andrew Brink and Arthur Mitzman are both American by birth. In terms of the training of psychohistorians, the overwhelming majority did their graduate training in the United States, including the majority of those from other countries. Eighteen took their doctoral degrees in history, eight in psychology, three each in literature and political science, and the rest in a variety of fields. Eighty percent are not psychoanalytically trained, with only eleven scholars receiving very extensive analytic training and two others undergoing some training. Some colleagues, including William McKinley Runyan, see themselves as coming from personality psychology and additional areas, as well as the psychoanalytic tradition. David Beisel, Mary Coleman, John Demos, and Lee Shneidman were influenced by their spouses being therapists or psychoanalysts. In terms of affiliations, there are four from UCLA, which constitutes the largest number from a single university; next, there are three each from Harvard, UC Berkeley, and York University. Two scholars are affiliated with each of the following institutions: Brandeis, U. of Toronto, UC Davis, *The Journal of Psychohistory*, Yale, U. of Amsterdam, U. of Maryland, and Princeton.[11]

In North America, the interviewees tended to—not surprisingly—be centered in the metropolitan areas of New York, Boston, Los Angeles, and San Francisco. Chicago and Toronto represent two other centers of psychohistory. In terms of religious origins, fifty-one percent are Jewish and forty-three percent are Christian. There is one Muslim and one Hindu in the group, and the backgrounds of three percent of the scholars are unknown. In terms of gender, eighty-four percent of my sample is male and sixteen percent female. It is noteworthy that generally psychohistory has not done an especially good job of bringing women into the ranks of its leadership. This is quite noticeable in the IPA.[12]

Certainly not all, and quite probably not a majority, of our featured scholars and editors identify themselves as psychohistorians, but all have done work that is very clearly psychohistorical. Lynn Hunt, for example, president of the American Historical Association in 2002, wrote a quite psychohistorically informed book on the French Revolution and welcomed being interviewed for a psychohistorical journal,[13] but does not see herself as a psychohistorian and indeed has distanced herself from psychohistory since her interview in 1998. Despite the enormous body of work that has been accomplished and the institutions created, psychohistory is a controversial field that has had many ups and downs.

Sometimes I have the impression that psychohistory is rather like religion was in the Soviet Union. It was condemned, suppressed, and shunned by the authorities that said that because the churchgoers were the gray-haired retirees, they would soon die out. They said that for generation after generation. However, ultimately it was the Communist system, rather than religion, that died out. Psychohistory awaits a new generation of scholars who are more steeped in the psychological language that has permeated our society and no longer have the prejudices of the older academic generation who will eventually die off. Colleagues know so little of the history of psychohistory that even distinguished psychohistorians like Robert Jay Lifton think that Isaac Asimov invented the term.[14] Very few individuals know that the term "psychohistory" was used by the 1920s, and that even in the first decade of the century there were psychobiographical studies.[15] In this book you will learn about the rich history of the field and my role in it as a historian interviewing leading colleagues and a participant-observer who uses the Eriksonian method of disciplined subjectivity.

Notes

1 There is a good article on psychohistory's history by two Finnish University of Helsinki authors, although the first one (Pietikainen) is an opponent of the field. Petteri Pietikainen and Juhani Ihanus, "On the Origins of Psychoanalytic Psychohistory," *History of Psychology*, Vol. 6 No. 2 (May 2003): pp. 171–914.

2 For definitions by Beisel, Binion, deMause, Hughes, Lawton, Loewenberg, Kren, Mazlish, Roazen, Strozier, Szaluta, and Volkan see Paul H. Elovitz, ed., *Psychohistory for the Twenty-First Century: The Best of the Journal Clio's Psyche* (2013): pp. 2–3.

3 Barbara Tuchman, "Response to deMause," *The Journal of Psychohistory*, Vol. 3 No. 2 (Fall 1975): p. 184. It is no accident that Tuchman was not an academic historian.

4 My edited books include *Historical and Psychological Inquiry* (1990), *Immigrant Experiences: Personal Narrative and Psychological Analysis* (1997; co-edited), four *Special Student Editions of Clio's Psyche* used in teaching, *Appearance and Reality* (2009), and *Psychohistory for the 21st Century* (2013).

5 Although I only met Vamık Volkan in person in passing, I have worked with him for many years as an admirer, editor, and scholar.

6 My use of the terms "honor" and "appreciate" should not lead the reader to think that I am inclined to idealize these and the other individuals I write about in Featured Scholar and Editor Interviews and obituaries. In my own writing and that of others who I ask to do these psychobiographical tasks, my goal is to present realistic pictures of the people under consideration.

7 As an advocate of disciplined subjectivity I have felt it necessary to not only privately, including in my personal analysis, examine my conscious and unconscious motivations, but also to be more open about my motivation in writing and presentations than is usually the case for historians. My somewhat negative transference to Erikson is based primarily on his failure to support the field of psychohistory, his belittling of Preserved Smith's role as a Luther scholar, his inadequacies as a father, and his rejection of his Judaism.

8 Lawrence J. Friedman, *Identity's Architect: A Biography of Erik H. Erikson* (1999); Paul Roazen, *Erik H. Erikson: The Power and Limits of a Vision* (1976); Robert Coles, *Erik H. Erikson: The Growth of His Work* (1970); Daniel Burston, *Erik Erikson and the American Psyche: Ego, Ethics, and Evolution* (2006). There are also numerous articles on Erikson, especially in the *Psychohistory Review*.

9 Early on I thought of doing a collective biography, a prosopographic study, but I realized that the time required for this was not compatible with my other obligations.

10 I dropped Castelloe and O'Keefe because they were interviewed specifically as "young psychohistorians" and the Featured Scholars are a much more distinguished group. From this study I also dropped Larry Shiner, who did a fine job as the last editor of the *Psychohistory Review*, but was a philosopher by training who never did psychohistory nor saw himself as a psychohistorian. I was considering dropping the MacArthur Award-winning Frank J. Sulloway from those being analyzed, but I realized, in a broad sense, that despite his rejection of Freud he has done some impressive psychohistory, especially in *Born to Rebel: Birth Order, Family Dynamics, and Creative Lives* (1996). In a July 24, 2017 telephone conversation, Professor Sulloway confirmed that in a general sense he is certainly a psychohistorian.

11 The affiliations are based primarily upon the time the individual was interviewed.

12 In forty years the IPA has only had one woman president, although other groups have done better. The APCS has very active female participation with a majority of women on the Board of Directors. The late Elisabeth Young-Bruehl was chair prior to the participation of Marilyn Charles who has been co-chair for many years, last year (2017) with another woman. Thus women are quite prominent in APCS leadership, including in its journal where Lynne Layton of Harvard was co-editor for an extended period.

13 Lynn Hunt, *The Family Romance of the French Revolution* (1992) and Bob Lentz, "Autonomy, the French Revolution, and Human Rights: Lynn Hunt," *Clio's Psyche*, Vol. 4 No. 4 (March 1998): pp. 110, 129–133.

14 Robert Jay Lifton, ed., *Explorations in Psychohistory: The Wellfleet Papers* (1974): p. 17. Lifton's *Witness to an Extreme Century: A Memoir* (2014), 76n, continues to imply that the term psychohistory was based on Asimov's predictive fantasy psychohistory.

15 Elizabeth W. Marvick and Paul H. Elovitz, "L. Pierce Clark: An Early Psychobiographer," *Clio's Psyche*, Vol. 17 No. 1–2 (June–September 2010): pp. 10–17.

2

MY EXUBERANT JOURNEY

As a young historian teaching at Temple University and as a graduate student writing my dissertation in the 1960s, I found psychoanalysis to be, like history, focused on origins and turning points. While historians tended to minimize the role of individuals, psychoanalysts are specifically concerned with them. As I devoured books on the unconscious and read all the psychobiographical studies of famous individuals available, I quickly became a psychological historian. My study, like that of many others drawn to the emerging field of psychohistory, was and is on childhood, collective fantasies, creativity, dreams, group dynamics, mechanisms of psychic defense (coping mechanisms), psychobiography, psychopolitics, psychoanthropology, and trauma.

Alexander and Juliette George's *Woodrow Wilson and Colonel House: A Personality Study* (1956) inspired me because of its insights and the fact that it reserved the psychological concepts for the afterword. Inspired by the work of the Georges, psychoanalytic insight without pathologizing the subject or introducing technical terminology became my mantra. Erik Erikson's *Young Man Luther* (1958) thrilled me because it brought in the emotions and turning points in the life of the originator of the Protestant Reformation, although I had doubts as to just how good a historian the author was, as pointed out by Reformation scholars.[1]

Robert Jay Lifton's much more factually based books, including *Death in Life: Survivors of Hiroshima* (1968), inspired me to learn by interviewing subjects as well as probing documents as I was taught to do in graduate school. Frank Manuel's *A Portrait of Sir Isaac Newton* (1968) excited me because it showed how a scientific genius could create a new paradigm and yet be obsessed by the old paradigm of Biblical studies. On the other hand, speculative volumes such as Abraham Bronson Feldman's *The Unconscious in History* (1959) made such broad, unsubstantiated generalizations based on theory rather than evidence that they left me cold and were skimmed rather than read.

My journey to psychohistory was based partly on accident, personal need, an intellectual movement, and a societal milieu. The accident was that I was teaching with a historian of ancient Rome named Sidney Halpern at the Ambler Campus of Temple University who had incredible insights based on wide reading of the psychoanalytic literature, some analytic training, a profound sense of the role of the unconscious in human affairs, and, not least of all, his brilliance. The personal need was that I was facing crises in my marital and personal life that could benefit from therapy, although at the time I did not consciously know this. I only knew that I had writer's block on my dissertation and that my new friend Sid Halpern would listen as I spoke about my research and then tell me what he heard. Only then did my ideas seem to be worthy of writing down. He also suggested various psychoanalytic readings, which I devoured.

The societal movement was a veneration of Freud, Erikson, and psychoanalysis, with the latter glorified in some Hollywood movies. Finally, the intellectual movement was a growing literature in applied psychoanalysis and a sense that psychohistory might become the next "big thing" in history. The call to younger historians to apply psychoanalysis to history as "the next assignment" by Harvard Professor William Langer in his 1957 Presidential Address to the American Historical Association seemed to be becoming a reality.

The integration of psychology into history and political science progressed rapidly and reached a tipping point in the early 1970s in what the distinguished psychohistorian David Beisel reports began to "look like a Golden Age" for psychological history.[2] Throughout the country, groups committed to studying applied psychoanalysis seemed to spring up overnight like mushrooms. The number of psychohistorical dissertations and articles increased remarkably.[3] There was a wave of anthologies, articles, journals, monographs, and groups (local, national, and international). Some academics went into psychoanalytic training, as I did several years later,[4] and psychohistorical courses sprang up like mushrooms overnight. I offered my first explicitly psychohistorical course in 1972. I read with rapt attention psychohistorical articles appearing in the *American Historical Review* and other mainstream journals, as I had for some time in psychoanalytic journals.[5] *The Journal of Interdisciplinary History* came into existence in 1970 and published psychohistorical articles throughout the decade. Specialized psychohistorical journals began in 1972 with the mimeographed *Newsletter of the Group for the Use of Psychology in History* and a full-fledged quarterly journal by 1978. *The History of Childhood Quarterly: The Journal of Psychohistory* (later *The Journal of Psychohistory*) began publication in 1973 as a substantial quarterly, and the editor reported 8,000 subscribers by the 1980s. I read the first issue that came into my hands from cover to cover. To call editor Lloyd deMause I used the excuse that one of the sources cited in an article on the impact of the English Industrial Revolution had been demonstrated to be spurious. He welcomed my concern and after a number of years I became a contributing editor of the journal. *Political Psychology*, the journal of the International Society for Political Psychology (ISPP), was launched in 1979 and contained some psychohistorically-based articles along with much academic political science and psychology.[6] I was far from alone in seeing psychohistory as the wave of the future.

Advocates of the new paradigm created explicit psychohistory organizations such as the Group for the Study of Psychohistorical Process in 1966, which met around Robert Jay Lifton's seminar tables in a shack outside his Wellfleet on Cape Cod summer home. Leading intellectuals assembled there annually for three-day conferences with initial funding from the American Academy of Arts and Sciences, which hoped it would become "a training center for psychohistorical work."[7] Psychohistory blossomed as an organized field in the 1970s in the U.S. with the establishment of a variety of organizations. The Group for the Use of Psychology in History (GUPH, 1972–1999) met at annual American Historical Association conferences.

In July 1975, Lloyd deMause's Institute for Psychohistory held its first three-day summer workshop. It was wonderful to be sitting around a conference table in a West Side New York City hotel with colleagues with similar interests. The prospect of eventually publishing in deMause's *The Journal of Psychohistory* was also enticing. The second workshop in 1976 was so inspiring to me and another participant that we suggested and then chaired bimonthly day-long Saturday meetings in the impressive conference room of deMause's publishing business at 2315 Broadway in New York City. I was learning from my fellow psychohistorians and thrilled by the prospect of understanding the history of childhood and the roots of violence as steps toward a world with healthier adults and less violence.

Attending the first national conference of psychohistorians in 1976 at Stockton College outside Atlantic City was enormously exciting because Lifton, Peter Loewenberg, Rudolph Binion, John Demos, deMause, Fred Weinstein, and other leaders of the emerging field were there. Some quite intellectualized colleagues were inclined to dominate the podium and neither Lifton nor deMause played a leadership role. Erik Erikson sent a message of encouragement. I remember coming away from the meeting thinking that ours was now a national movement and that it was important to actually do psychohistory rather than focus on its parameters. Advocates began to think internationally, thus the International Psychohistorical Association (IPA, 1977–) held its first annual conference in 1978 with most presenters being historians. The following week the International Society for Political Psychology (ISPP, 1977–) met for the first time and quickly became the largest and most truly international of these groups.[8] As discussed in the next chapter, psychohistorical studies were being written in both Europe and America for a half century before the establishment of a formal movement.

Notes

1 Roger A. Johnson, ed., *Psychohistory and Religion: The Case of Young Man Luther* (Philadelphia: Fortress Press, 1977).
2 David R. Beisel, "The Nazi Youth Cohort," *Clio's Psyche*, Vol. 19 No. 1 (June 2012): p. 108.

3 William McKinley Runyan, "From the Study of Lives and Psychohistory to Historicizing Psychology: A Conceptual Journey," in Jerome Winer and James Anderson, eds., *The Annual of Psychoanalysis: Special Issue on Psychoanalysis and History* (2003): p. 126, made an attempt to quantify the growth of psychohistorical literature. By title, he found the following results: "In 1965–1969, 12 dissertations, 65 books, and 150 articles; and in 1975–1979, 65 dissertations, 122 books, and 428 articles."

4 Paul H. Elovitz, "A Unique Dual Education: Editor's Introduction and Personal Commentary," *Clio's Psyche*, Vol. 4 No. 2 (September 1997): pp. 36–44. This issue includes articles by the dually trained Mark Bracher, John Fitzpatrick, Thomas Kohut, Peter Loewenberg, Jonathan Goldberg, Jeffrey Prager, Nellie Thompson, Richard Weiss, and Richard Wolfenstein. The featured scholar interview in the issue was of the dual trained Peter Gay. The partially trained Lloyd deMause wrote "From Hitler to Historical Evolution," describing how he was asked to leave the National Psychological Association for Psychoanalysis (NPAP) training program because he wanted to analyze Hitler, rather than living patients. A few of these individuals had trained before the 1970s and many would train after this period. Unless historians were well established in history departments prior to training in psychoanalysis, they were unlikely to get tenure because of the weak market for historians and prejudices against psychohistory. Consequently, like the talented European intellectual historian David James Fisher, they are inclined to make their living as clinicians.

5 Such as *American Imago, The Psychoanalytic Quarterly, The Psychoanalytic Study of the Child,* and *The Annual of Psychoanalysis.*

6 The number of journals publishing psychohistory was noteworthy in this period. Psychobiographical articles continued to be published in *American Imago, The Psychoanalytic Quarterly, The Psychoanalytic Study of the Child, The Annual of Psychoanalysis, The Journal of Interdisciplinary History* (1970–circa 1980) and various other journals published psychobiographical articles. Specialized psychohistorical articles began in 1972 with the mimeographed *Newsletter of the Group for the Use of Psychology in History* that was transformed into a quarterly journal by 1978. In 1973, *The History of Childhood Quarterly: The Journal of Psychohistory* (in 1978 the name was changed to *The Journal of Psychohistory*) was published by Lloyd deMause and has always been a profitable and substantial quarterly. Additional journals are *Clio's Psyche* (1994–); *Mind and Human Interaction* (1989–2005); *The Psychohistory News: Newsletter of the International Psychohistorical Association* (1978–); *Mentalities/Mentalités* (1981–2011); *Or le temps: Revue Francaise de Psychohistorie* (1994–2000); *Psicologica Politica* (1990–); *Journal for the Psychoanalysis of Culture and Society* (1995–); *Psychoanalysis and History* (1999–); and *Gesellschaft für Psychohistorie und Politische Psychologie* (1993–). None of these have had as much circulation as *The Journal of Psychohistory*. The readers of the *American Historical Review* did not like reading articles based on Freudian theory. For example, Otto Pflanze's 1972 *AHR* article on Bismarck as a phallic personality was an extremely insightful article based on extraordinarily revealing sources, but it was too overtly Freudian to be readily accepted by most historians.

7 Lifton, *Witness*, p. 344.

8 The ISPP was much less psychoanalytically and psychohistorically based, although it did have psychoanalyst/psychohistorians like Vamık Volkan, its fourth president, as active members. In terms of its membership size, it has always been much more successful than the IPA, in part because it moved its meetings around the country and the world, unlike the IPA, which has only had one meeting outside of New York City. The ISPP has a very active early career scholars program.

3

THE EARLY HISTORY OF PSYCHOHISTORY

The first use I have found of the word "psycho-historical" was in an August 25, 1840 letter by the American Romantic poet, critic, editor, and diplomat James Russell Lowell (1819–1891).[1]

Interest in psychology was growing in the late nineteenth century, and by the twentieth century some individuals were beginning to consider applying it to society and history. Some Americans, especially the Boston School, were influenced by developments in Europe and led in this endeavor, which was related to the interest in psychotherapy and the unconscious. I was thrilled to discover that as early as 1909 and 1912 Morton Prince did rudimentary studies of Kaiser Wilhelm II of Germany and President Roosevelt. Sigmund Freud's 1909 Clark lectures heightened interest in psychoanalysis and the application of it to society.

Sigmund Freud deserves enormous credit for providing the groundwork for applied psychoanalysis, political psychology, psychobiography, and psychohistory. The creator of psychoanalysis' focus on the individual and insights into the unconscious were essential to these subsequent developments. However, Freud was not himself a psychohistorian, and his various attempts at psychohistory were either extremely speculative or seriously flawed. The founder of psychoanalysis never used the words "psychohistory" or "psychobiography."[2] Of course, as is well known, he did try his hand at both psychobiography and psychohistory, most notably of Leonardo da Vinci and Moses. However, he was apologetic about the flaws in these works. Freud used the terms "applied psychoanalysis" and "applied psychology" for what we would call psychohistory or psychobiography.[3] Applied psychoanalysis flourished in the Freud circle among the mostly medical individuals, who as Europeans were steeped in history. In addition, as they were developing new psychoanalytic knowledge, at times it was safer to diagnose historical personages than to refer to cases because most individuals in the analytic community were known to each other. Some rudimentary psychobiography and psychohistory may be found in the *Minutes of the Vienna Psychoanalytic Society* and elsewhere. There were early studies on Amenhotep IV (1912), Louis Bonaparte (1914), Dante (1914), del Sarto (1913), Ebner (1910), Gogol (1912), Lenau (1909), Loyola (1913), Napoleon (1914), Segantini (1911), Shakespeare (1910), Schopenhauer (1913), von Kleist (1910), Wagner (1911), Zinzendorf (1910), and others. The authors were Karl Abraham, Max Graf, Eduard Hitschmann, Ludwig Jekels, Ernest Jones, Otto Kaus, Georg Lomer, Oskar Pfister, Otto Rank, Isidor Sadger, and Alice Sperber.[4] Many appeared in the journal *Imago* that Freud established. His *Leonardo Da Vinci and a Memory of His Childhood* (1910) is better than most studies from his period, but deeply flawed.

It was exciting for me to learn that in 1913 in America, the Reformation historian Preserved Smith published "Luther's Early Development in the Light of Psycho-analysis," which probed childhood, obsession with the devil, and sexual desire in a fine piece of work for the period.[5] Elizabeth Marvick, my co-author in an article on Smith, credits him with having "integrated psychoanalytic hypothesis into his perspectives."[6] However, his fellow historians were not enthusiastic about this approach, and he never again wrote explicitly psychological history. It seemed wrong to me that most colleagues thought that it was Erik Erikson who first wrote about Luther's psychodynamics. James Harvey Robinson advocated the "new history," which focused on analysis as well as description and drew materials from psychology as well as economics. He was an associate editor of the *American Historical Review* (1912–1920) and subsequently president of the American Historical Association (1929), but he did not personally write any explicit psychohistory. Advocates are important, but it is the practitioners whom I most value.

The most prolific of the early authors applying psychoanalysis to history was L. Pierce Clark, a New York City neurologist and psychoanalyst, who started writing on psychoanalysis in 1908. He applied Freud's ideas to famous individuals, genius, Greek art, and epilepsy with considerable energy. His subjects included Akhenaton, Alexander the Great, Caesar, Leonardo da Vinci, Dostoevsky, Napoleon, Lincoln, and Michelangelo.[7] By the third decade of the century he was using the terms "psychohistory" and "psychobiography," with and without a hyphen. Although he does not appear to have done much original research, because he avoided technical psychoanalytic language and wrote about famous individuals such as Lincoln and Napoleon, his writings reached a lay audience.[8] He published *The Archives of Psychoanalysis* in 1926–1927, which had an impressive array of articles and books by European analysts from Freud to Georg Groddeck and Wilhelm Reich, as well as his own work. Clark died unexpectedly at age fifty-three with his *New York Times* obituary headlining that Lincoln's mother had "a lifelong influence" on the president. To our generation this seems simplistic, but it reflects the application of Freudian ideas to historical personages.

In my search for early advocates of psychological history, I was shocked to discover Harry Elmer Barnes, the Holocaust denier. I knew that he had been a promising historian before his pro-German World War I revisionism led him to denial. I wondered if he could be a case of a rebel who came to my field precisely because it was on the fringes of acceptability. Whatever the cause, early in his career Barnes was intrigued by the application of psychology to history, although his definition of psychology was quite broad. His 1919 and 1921 articles, "Psychology and History: Some Reasons for Predicting Their More Active Cooperation in the Future" and "Some Reflections on the Possible Service of Analytical Psychology to History," were, like Preserved Smith's study on Luther, published in psychological rather than historical journals.[9] The academic psychologist Franklin Fearing (1892–1962) in 1927 wrote positively about the genre of the new psychobiography.[10]

In the 1920s, the idea of merging psychology and history was reaching a larger number of intellectuals, though much less so the reality. The growth of interest in our subject matter can be traced by going through William Gilmore's *Psychohistorical Inquiry: A Comprehensive Research Bibliography* (1984).[11] By the 1940s, among the authors who became well known contributors were the Americans Abram Kardiner and Karl Menninger, the English-American Geoffrey Gorer, and the German-Americans Erik Erikson and Erich Fromm. Sydney Ratner, with whom I studied economic history at Rutgers University, wrote "The Historian's Approach to Psychology," but quickly lost interest in the field.[12] Because I knew him to be such an out-of-touch-with-reality, absent-minded professor, I am glad he did not follow through on this interest.

During World War II, General William "Wild Bill" Donovan of the Office of Strategic Services (OSS)—the predecessor to the CIA—recognized the value of knowing his enemy when he enlisted psychoanalysts Walter Langer, Henry A. Murray, and others to interview captured German soldiers and others who had contact with Hitler to write a secret history of the Third Reich's leader.[13] Despite the difficulties with sources and the countertransference issues evoked by writing dispassionately about one's enemy during wartime, there was much of value in the report that was eventually declassified and published as *The Mind of Adolf Hitler* (1972). Langer was so enthused by this methodology that he offered to write a similar study on Stalin, but the idea was dismissed out of hand because the Russian "man of steel" was our ally and the methodology was only seen as appropriate for enemies.[14] Subsequently, the CIA hired a large array of colleagues to research and write reports on both major leaders and obscure and possible leaders.

The émigré influence on the development of psychohistory in America is considerable. Erich Fromm's *Escape from Freedom* (1941) was first published in England as *The Fear of Freedom* and continues to be read, especially as democracies are threatened in the twenty-first century. His "On the Problem of German Characterology" has had an impact, but not as much as Erik Homburger Erikson's 1942 "Hitler's Imagery and German Youth."[15] Erikson's 1958 *Young Man Luther* was the first widely acclaimed psychohistory book, which has resulted in many viewing him as the father of our field.[16] This accolade never sat well with Erich Fromm, who was much more prolific and had a wider audience as both a popular author of applied psychoanalysis and perhaps as a serious scholar, including his monumental *The Anatomy of Human Destructiveness* (1973).[17] I found Erikson's explicit psychohistory to be much more readable than Fromm's.

Erik H. Erikson (1902–1994) was a refugee from Nazi Europe who became an American cultural icon. He played a key role in the origins of the modern psychohistorical movement—a movement he was reluctant to involve himself in. He is mostly known for developing the concept of identity, which grew out of his need to find his own identity. This was the situation because his mother, Karla Abrahamson, a Danish Jew with connections in Germany, became pregnant and never told her son the name of his natural father, which she may not have known. In Germany his mother married a Jewish physician, but tall, blonde, blue-eyed Erik did not feel or look Jewish and thought of himself as the son of a Scandinavian aristocrat, often visiting his Danish relatives. He seems to have experienced his stepfather as an intruder in his relationship with his mother. The young boy was told that his short, kindly, Jewish-looking stepfather, whose name of Homburger he was given, was his biological father, which was contradicted by their very different looks and characteristics. Young Erik knew something was amiss, which began his search for his birth father and identity. In the synagogue, which he did not like, his nickname was "goy" based on his looks.[18] Nor did the artistic boy enjoy the Gymnasium with its focus on classical Greek, Latin, and literature. He was at best an average student, and upon completing it he had no interest in going to university.

Almost seven years of wanderlust followed for Erik Homburger. He hiked, went to art school for a while, and seemed a failure to his stepfather. Lawrence J. Friedman in *Identity's Architect: A Biography of Erik H. Erikson* (1999) shows how most of this talented man's many theories can be related to his struggle for identity and life experiences. Unsure if he was a Dane or German, Jew or Gentile, analyst or artist, Homburger forged his own way. In turning his struggles into theories, he broadened our understanding of how people see themselves. Erik Homburger would rename, and thus re-identify, himself as Erik H. Erikson, going back to his search for a Danish father for whom he longed but would never find or even be certain existed. His years of uncertainty led him to see somewhat similar wanderings in others he studied, thus his concept of the psychosocial moratorium.

It was in Vienna, where he was invited by his friend Peter Blos, who was setting up a school for children of Freud's patients, that he found his way as a teacher as well as an analysand of Anna Freud and ultimately a child analyst. Partly because of his playfulness, Erik was more comfortable with children, with whom he was inclined to have a special connection, than with adults. Although he became an analyst, it was with a minimum of psychoanalytic training, and he was ambivalent about his own limited analysis with Anna Freud. Indeed, after he fell in love with

Joan Serson, a Canadian dancer, there was a tension in his mind regarding these two women. Not surprisingly, he felt much closer to the woman he would live with and eventually marry than to his analyst. Erikson's connection with Joan, who had already renamed herself as he would rename himself later in America, was very powerful. Each sought to reinvent themselves, and in doing this they separated themselves from others. A restlessness pervaded Erikson's life, which took him to many different places, including Yale, Harvard, the University of California, and Austen Riggs in the United States. It was not easy for him to fit in, but he found allies, and with the help of Joan and friends like Margaret Mead, he became a cultural icon.

For a man who was rather unsure of himself, becoming a cultural leader was rather surprising. Erikson would defend his status as, in a sense, the psychoanalyst to the nation, partly by covering ways in which he and his family were imperfect. Thus when his wife, who was temporarily incapacitated, gave birth to a Down's Syndrome child, the baby was immediately institutionalized and kept as a secret from his children and society. His daughter Sue writes about the cost of fame and Erik being "an awkward father," distant from even family members. She was desperate for attention, and her father feared that her unhappiness as a young child would spoil the image of the perfect family that he cultivated.[19] Simultaneously, Erikson was inspiring his students at Harvard.

Clearly Erikson's work on Hitler, various Native American groups, Luther, Gandhi, and various ages of the life cycle is important. Early on he stressed his view that Hitler was not a father figure, as most psychoanalysts who wrote about him thought, but the leader of the gang. Erikson had presented this view to the predecessor to the CIA, and it would ultimately be published in his *Childhood and Society* (1950). Unfortunately, as Friedman writes, Erikson was "uninterested in leading or participating in the psychohistorical movement."[20]

The personalities and values of leaders and their capacity to improve or harm their society is of great importance and interest. Deceased presidents and leaders have been fair game for amateur historians, especially in retirement, coming from medicine and a variety of other fields, resulting in psychobiographies of most uneven value. Their tendency has been to pathologize presidents and other leaders. From the beginning of psychohistory to the present, the field has had an abundance of simplistic studies, such as L. Pierce Clark's *Napoleon: Self Destroyed* (1929).

In the first two decades after the Second World War, it was the blossoming of psychoanalysis in America that made possible the rapid development of psychohistorical studies in the 1960s and '70s. Freud was hailed by intellectuals, Hollywood films presented psychoanalysis in a favorable fashion, and among some cultural leaders it became fashionable to go into analysis.

Most people first learned the term "psychohistory" from Isaac Asimov's science fiction, in which a psychohistorian could predict the future with mathematical precision. The World War II Office of Strategic Services' (OSS) psychological study of Hitler had correctly predicted his suicide. Its successor, the Central Intelligence Agency (CIA), hired numerous analysts to try to predict the behavior of leaders and potential leaders around the globe. The absence of much data from Stalinist Russia encouraged psychological interpretations and speculations by scholars such as Geoffrey Gorer and Nathan Leites.

History and psychology were integrated at an accelerated pace from the 1950s through the '60s and '70s. The results were articles, books, anthologies, journals, and college courses. Local study groups in applied psychoanalysis sprang up, followed by national and international organizations. Anthropologists and other academics began to train in psychoanalysis. Academic psychologists rejected this development, while clinicians joined it in large numbers. Although some leaders of the historical profession encouraged this development, history departments as a whole were opposed. The initial path-breaking psychohistorical studies that were beginning to inspire some young historians were by persons outside of the historical field.

William L. Langer sought to break through the "iron curtain" separating historians from "dynamic psychologists" when he gave his 1957 Presidential Address to the American Historical Association. This distinguished diplomatic historian and chair of Harvard's history department, whose psychiatrist brother, Walter, was the author of the OSS study of Hitler, made a well-reasoned and thoughtful argument. He pointed out that "the homespun, common-sense psychological interpretations of past historians" appear as "woefully inadequate," even "naïve" in contrast to psychodynamic knowledge.[21] Although there was grumbling in the audience by some of his colleagues, younger historians began to consider the idea.[22] While he recognized that it was "professionally dangerous" to do so, he nevertheless called for younger historians to take up the torch.

Publications by historians who responded in the 1960s were Bruce Mazlish's *Psychoanalysis and History* (edited, 1963), Rudolph Binion's *Frau Lou: Nietzsche's Wayward Disciple* (1968; a brilliant but flawed study), Frank Manuel's *A Portrait of Sir Isaac Newton* (1969), and Arthur Mitzman's *The Iron Cage: An Historical Interpretation of Max Weber* (1969). Note that psychobiographies were the primary genre produced. The scene was set for the explosion of psychohistorical knowledge and opportunities in the 1970s that changed my life, as well as produced a strong reaction against psychohistory.

Notes

1   Charles Elliot Norton, ed., *Letters of James Russell Lowell* Vol. 1 (New York: Harper Brothers Publishers, 1894): p. 60. Subsequently I hope to write a short article on the early use of the terms "psychobiography" and "psychohistory."
2   This is easy to verify by checking Samuel Guttmann, et al., eds., *The Concordance of the Standard Edition of the Complete Psychological Works of Sigmund Freud* (Boston: G.K. Hall, 1980).

3 Alan Elms, "Sigmund Freud: Psychohistorian," in Jerome Wiener and James Anderson, eds., *Psychoanalysis and History* (2006): pp. 65–78, presents a more favorable view of Freud as a historian than most colleagues.

4 Lucile Dooley, "Psychoanalytic Studies of Genius," *The American Journal of Psychology*, Vol. 27 No. 3 (July 1916): pp. 363–416.

5 P. Smith, "Luther's Early Development in the Light of Psycho-Analysis," *The American Journal of Psychology*, Vol. 24 (1913): pp. 360–377.

6 Elizabeth W. Marvick and Paul H. Elovitz, "America's First Psychobiographer: Preserved Smith and His Insights on Luther," *Clio's Psyche*, Vol. 17 No. 1–2 (2010): pp. 22–28. In designating America's first psychobiographer, priority was given to Smith rather than Prince because of his greater depth of knowledge and sophistication and the fact that he published in a journal rather than a newspaper.

7 Elizabeth W. Marvick and Paul H. Elovitz, "L. Pierce Clark: An Early Psychobiographer," *Clio's Psyche*, Vol. 17 No. 1–2 (June–September 2010): pp. 10–17.

8 Clark's psychohistorical books are *Napoleon Self-Destroyed* (1929) and *Lincoln: A Psychobiography* (1933).

9 Respectively in *The American Journal of Psychology*, Vol. 30 No. 4 (1919): pp. 337–376 and the *Psychoanalytic Review*, Vol. 8 (1921): pp. 22–37.

10 Franklin Fearing, "Psychological Studies of Historical Personalities," *Psychological Bulletin*, Vol. 24 No. 9 (September 1927): pp. 521–539.

11 Gilmore's *Psychohistorical Inquiry: A Comprehensive Research Bibliography* is an invaluable aide that needs updating because it omitted a significant number of sources and included too broad a definition of psychohistory. The historical sketch in William McKinley Runyan, *Life Histories and Psychobiography: Explorations in Theory and Method* (New York: Oxford University Press, 1984): pp. 193–195, is worth consulting.

12 Sidney Ratner, "The Historian's Approach to Psychology," *Journal of the History of Ideas*, Vol. 2 (1941): pp. 95–109.

13 Henry A. Murray, *Analysis of the Personality of Adolf Hitler With Predictions of His Future Behavior and Suggestions For Dealing With Him Now and After Germany's Surrender* (1943). Walter Langer's older brother William was head of the research and analysis section of the Office of Strategic Services. Murray's report was suppressed during the war, but is now available online.

14 Subsequently, the Princeton University political scientist and historian Robert Tucker wrote numerous books on Stalin and the Soviet system he dominated. See especially *Stalin as Revolutionary: 1879–1929* (1988) and *Stalin in Power: The Revolution from Above, 1928–1941* (1990). Psychoanalysis was a major influence on Tucker, although his Wikipedia article makes no reference to psychohistory.

15 Erich Fromm, "On the Problems of German Characterology," *Transactions of the New York Academy of Sciences*, Vol. 5 (1943): pp. 79–83; Erik H. Erikson, "Hitler's Imagery and German Youth," *Psychiatry: Journal for the Study of Interpersonal Processes*, Vol. 5 (1942): pp. 475–493. Gustav Bychowski (1895–1972) was an émigré who wrote on political leaders, but with much less impact. For example, "Oliver Cromwell and the Puritan Revolution: A Chapter on the Psychology of Dictatorship," *Journal of Clinical and Experimental Psychology and the Quarterly Review of Psychiatry*, Vol. 7 (1945): pp. 281–309.

16 Personally, I see Erikson as only one of the fathers of the psychohistory movement, certainly not "the father."

17 See Lawrence J. Friedman, *The Lives of Erich Fromm: Love's Prophet* (New York: Columbia University Press, 2013). Among his eight books Friedman has fine psychobiographies on Erik H. Erikson and the Menningers.

18 Lawrence J. Friedman, *Identity's Architect: A Biography of Erik H. Erikson* (1999): p. 38.

19 Sue Erikson Bloland, *In the Shadow of Fame: A Memoir by the Daughter of Erik H. Erikson* (2005): pp. 14, 30. His daughter, also a psychoanalyst, presented at the Psychohistory Forum as well as at Ramapo's history club.

20 *Identity's Architect*, p. 271.

21 W. L. Langer, "The Next Assignment," *The American Historical Review*, Vol. 63 No. 2 (1958): p. 284.

22 See Peter Loewenberg, *Decoding the Past: The Psychohistorical Approach* (Berkeley: University of California Press, 1983), especially the chapter on the Langer brothers to better understand the personal roots of Langer's call to psychohistorical action.

4

RESISTANCE AND PERSEVERANCE

My first memory of hearing a professor use the word "psychohistory" was in a 1962 Rutgers University graduate history course on the Renaissance and Reformation, in which a fellow student wanted to do a psychohistorical study. Professor Donald Weinstein sneered at him, denounced the field, and contemptuously declared that if he wanted to do psychohistory he should go to Harvard, presumably because that is where William Langer taught.[1] The student received a poor grade and soon left the university. While I have a mild demeanor and tendency not to be a rebel, I am a determined person and knew that there must be something to psychohistory despite the professor's denunciation. If it was good enough for Harvard there must be something of value in it. Five or six years after this denunciation of psychohistory, when I was teaching at Temple University, I read Frank Manuel's *Newton* with pleasure, and on a trip back to Rutgers, I asked a professor I met in passing what he thought of it. He hadn't read it but remarked that it seemed like a good book according to the reviews. It was a relief to know that not all the faculty was like my Renaissance Reformation professor.

The mantra of graduate students and young professors was "publish or perish." This ran counter to my idealistic belief at the time that caring about students should preclude primarily putting energies into publishing. I was so disillusioned with the atmosphere of Temple University with its eighty-three-person history department that I referred to it as an education factory with unpainted cinderblock walls without soft music being piped into the classrooms (as was then a trend in factories). My colleagues spoke mostly of publications and college politics rather than of students, and the students in my courses seemed far more interested in meeting general education requirements than in knowledge. After two years, I was so frustrated that I quit Temple to take a poorly paid one-year research fellowship at Rutgers to work on my dissertation. I did much more research, but no writing, and I needed a better paying job to support my wife and three young children.

The chair of Temple University generously rehired me, suggesting that I might want to teach at the bucolic Ambler Campus in the suburbs of Philadelphia.[2] I jumped at the opportunity, which proved to be transformational because in Ambler I discovered both psychoanalysis and psychohistory, received encouragement in writing my dissertation, and loved the small campus atmosphere where I felt I could make a difference without publishing. Before I "perished" because I had not published, I helped my friend and fellow professor, Sid Halpern, become dean of the campus and knew that my future lay not in an impersonal university, but in a small interdisciplinary college.

Ramapo College was created as an interdisciplinary college in northern New Jersey at just the right time for me to be hired as one of the founding faculty members in 1971. Because I was bubbling over with enthusiasm for my new knowledge, the chair of our interdisciplinary division suggested I offer a psychohistory course in the summer. I loved teaching it. However, a historian and psychologist were trying together to undermine psychohistory, our chair (the first woman in a position of academic leadership in the college), and me by turning two of my students against my innovative first psychohistory course. (Ironically the two antagonistic colleagues shortly afterwards team-taught a course with psychology and history in the title, although it was nothing like my integration of psychology and history, and they never taught it again.) Subsequently, opponents of psychohistory tried to block me from receiving tenure, but failed because of overwhelming student support for my pedagogy.

Around the country, explicit psychohistory courses were springing up, although most of them did not continue into the late 1980s and beyond. David Beisel at Rockland SUNY was a notable exception; he taught psychohistory to over eight thousand students before retiring in 2016. His popularity as a professor teaching psychohistory saved his career when other colleagues were being de-tenured. At the International Psychohistorical Association (IPA), usually with Beisel, I gave workshops on teaching psychohistory in the 1970s and '80s. In the twenty-first century, due to Ramapo becoming less interdisciplinary and changes in requirements, I found less scope for psychohistorical teaching.[3] In a statement of professional identity, I had my title changed to Associate Professor of History, Psychohistory, and Interdisciplinary Studies.[4]

Regrettably, most academic historians have never warmed up to an overtly psychological approach.[5] They prefer to rely on their own insights as amateur psychologists often without even recognizing that they are making psychological assessments. In the twenty-first century, many historians don't even seem to know that psychohistory exists. Most historians are aware of it but pay little attention to it. Some who adamantly oppose it see psychohistory as a reductionist pathologizing of individuals, rather than a careful investigation of the childhood, coping mechanisms, creativity, emotions, overcoming of trauma, and personality, as well as the investigation of the difference between actual behavior and conscious intention.[6] There is sometimes an equation of psychohistory with psychoanalysis on which much, but far from all, psychohistory is based. Psychohistory is accused of being ahistorical, unscientific, and unverifiable. Freud is often devalued.[7]

These attacks on Freud and psychohistory are quite at variance with what I experienced. The Freud I learned about from my own group and personal analysis, intensive reading, eight years of psychoanalytic training, ten years of supervised analysis of my clinical work, and over a quarter century of analytic practice, focused on listening carefully to my patients rather than hanging labels on them. In my psychobiographies and psychohistories I seldom use technical terminology and fight reductionism wherever I can. As a result of considerable academic resistance, after the strong interest in the 1970s and early '80s among younger historians, over time the majority of advocates and practitioners of psychohistory come from anthropology, literature, political science, social work, sociology, and especially therapeutic settings. The struggles were not simply for psychohistory, but within psychohistory itself.

My conception of psychohistory eventually failed to fit in well with Lloyd deMause's impatient desire to create a separate scientific field of psychohistory based on his evolving theories. Our differences came to a head in the fall of 1982 when some members of the Institute's Saturday group and I discovered that we were locked out of our meeting place in the offices of deMause's business in Manhattan. His response was, "Casper [Schmidt] was supposed to unlock the door to my offices for your seminar. We are also going to discontinue the small groups in favor of large group outreach." I was shocked but determined to hold the meeting for the presenter who had traveled from New England to present his research. Eventually, the door was unlocked, the meeting was held, and my friend, the independent scholar Henry Lawton, and I started planning a psychohistorical group modeled after what we had done under the auspices of the Institute for Psychohistory, without sometimes advocating for particular theories or occasionally being unduly critical of some presenters. This was the origin of the Psychohistory Forum, which first met in the office of a women's psychohistory group and then in a variety of other venues, including mental health conference rooms, apartments of psychoanalysts in New York (some of which were quite elegant with beautiful skyline views of Manhattan), and at New York and Fordham Universities. The Forum remains active today and publishes *Clio's Psyche*. Lloyd deMause referred colleagues to Forum meetings and, for as long as his health allowed him to be active in the field, we cooperated in the interests of psychohistory.[8]

There are many reasons psychohistory did not harness the enormous enthusiasm to become an established field in history departments and elsewhere in academia. First and foremost, when a new field, such as economic history, is put forth, there is major opposition, but its advocates train their doctoral students who are hired elsewhere and then help establish it throughout academia. However, psychohistory became an organized field precisely during the jobs crises of the 1970s when history departments were more likely to de-tenure rather than hire new faculty. Charles Strozier reports that he was the only person hired as a psychohistorian. This was at Sangamon State University, which was created in 1971. Some younger historians, such as David Beisel,[9] Bill Gilmore, Strozier, and I,[10] advocated for the new field and tried to establish it in academia without the support of more established colleagues and failed. A few older colleagues, such as Peter Loewenberg at UCLA and George Kren, along with the psychologist Leon Rappoport at Kansas State University, had some short-term success before their ultimate failure to permanently establish psychohistory as an academic discipline.[11]

Furthermore, Erik Erikson and Robert Jay Lifton, the two most prominent psychohistorians of the late 1960s, were not historians and did not think psychohistory should be a separate field. Strozier grew discouraged by the lack of acceptance and terminated publication of *The Psychohistory Review* in 1999 because the editor of it and he were "tired of it" and more fundamentally thought "that psychohistory was never going to be recognized within the discipline of history as more than ephemeral . . . [with] very few people" having appointments in the field. At about the same time, GUPH ceased to meet.[12]

Splits among advocates of psychohistory were a secondary factor. The GUPH always disliked deMause and vice versa. He was both much too radical in his conception of the field and not diplomatic enough as an editor and in dealing with academic colleagues. Within the first five or six years of the establishment of *The Journal of Psychohistory* in 1973, prominent colleagues such as John Demos, Peter Loewenberg, Elizabeth Marvick, Bruce Mazlish, and Edward Shorter withdrew from the Editorial Board.[13] Most academic historians committed to the field wanted nothing to do with deMause and those associated with him, as I discovered as an organizer of meetings. There were feelings of us versus them encouraged by the different psychohistory organizations. In the week following our first meeting, I remember feeling somewhat disloyal to the IPA when I briefly attended the International Society for Political Psychology (ISPP) convention. Disgruntled IPA members like Jacques Szaluta often went to this organization.

Lloyd deMause was institution building while this was occurring. His Psychohistory Press was publishing books, the Saturday meetings were thriving, and the IPA was meeting annually and sometimes twice a year. DeMause listed a growing number of national and international branches of the Institute for Psychohistory, although most of these branches existed only on paper as the result of a foreign colleague expressing interest in psychohistory. He poured profits of the *Journal* into massive advertising campaigns. Despite the rivalries and excessive claims, significant psychohistorical work was being done in the institutions deMause had created. Furthermore, his commitment to building the field was unwavering, as opposed to the ambivalence of many associated with the GUPH.

As academic historians closed ranks against it, the practitioners of psychohistory became more multidisciplinary and different psychohistorical organizations proliferated. The Center on Violence and Human Survival was created in New

York City in 1986, and the Center for the Study of Mind and Human Interaction was created in 1987—with the companion journal *Mind and Human Interaction*. The Group for the Psychohistorical Study of Film was formed in 1989. In 1991, the University of California Psychoanalytic Consortium was formed, and in the early 1990s the East Bay Psychobiography Group came into existence. Increasingly, academics from a variety of departments joined with clinicians and in one case formed a new organization, the Association for the Psychoanalysis of Culture and Society (APCS), in 1994.[14] This group now meets every fall and has a valuable conference at Rutgers University, which includes colleagues from around the country and the U.K. In Boston, a group formed in the late 1980s around Paul Roazen, a prolific political scientist who wrote quite extensively about psychoanalysis and psychoanalysts. It met in the Harvard Club for dinner and a lecture followed by discussion. Following Roazen's death in 2005, it continues to meet regularly, for about five years in the Harvard Club and subsequently in the home of a psychoanalyst.[15] I suspect that there may be similar groups around North America that I simply do not know about. Today, psychohistory is diffused through academia, clinical settings, and popular scholarship as a truly interdisciplinary field that is not necessarily even recognizable to the users for what it is.

The "alleged death of psychohistory" is something that I occasionally read about as I continue my work with so many others in nurturing a field that has brought so much insight to the world. In 2014 my chapter, "The Successes and the Obstacles to the Interdisciplinary Marriage of Psychology and History," was published by Cambridge University Press in *Psychology and History*.[16] The editors were quite professional and a pleasure to work with. Unfortunately, in a volume on psychology and history that I anticipated being all about psychohistory, mine was the only chapter of the thirteen published that focused on psychohistory. Another argued that psychoanalysis and history are incommensurate.[17] A third author, Assistant Professor Rob Boddice, declared that psychohistory is "a defunct sub-discipline" of history because "historians' brief dalliance with psychohistory" is over.[18] In reading this, I was reminded of Alfred Nobel (1833–1896) reading his own obituary in 1888, as well as of Bertrand Russell reading his 1920 death notice, a full half century before his actual death. The question becomes, "What motivates Boddice's denial of our existence?" In his case, aside from ignorance, it is a commitment to "making emotions accessible to the historian."[19] Part of Boddice's scholarly focus is on compassion—of which he has none for those of us who do psychological history. In fact, psychohistory does a much better job of getting to emotions and their meaning than an abstract study of the emotions does.

One way academic historians have tried to sidestep psychohistory has been to focus on the history of emotions. Peter Stearns, who has published at least thirty-six books, more on the emotions than anything else, has been a leader in this endeavor. When he presented at the Psychohistory Forum in 1991, I was impressed with his encyclopedic knowledge of social and emotional history and embarrassed by the low turnout. Apparently our members had correctly predicted that this Carnegie Mellon University (now George Mason) professor would not be providing much depth of analysis. Separating the emotions from the people expressing them just doesn't provide the same insight as does psychoanalytically-based psychohistory. This was apparent in the case of a young social historian hired at Ramapo who taught a course on the history of childhood when his own children were young, but soon lost interest in it, perhaps because the personalities and psychodynamics of the families and children involved did not shine through the generalizations. He once made a gratuitously anti-Freud comment at a history meeting, which I challenged him on after the group left. Since then, he has been a good colleague who politely apologized for the anti-Freudianism that had been taught to him in graduate school as gospel.

Recently, Peter Loewenberg commented to me that psychohistory has lost the "flash" it had in the 1970s and '80s. But more importantly, it has not lost its depth of insight, which is what keeps us doing it.

Notes

1   Donald Weinstein (1926–2015), a leading scholar of the Italian Renaissance, did not get tenure at Rutgers and spent the rest of his career at the University of Arizona where he remained an outspoken critic of psychological history. While Langer was an advocate of psychohistory, I don't think that he actually taught courses on it.

2   My Temple salary as a lecturer and then assistant professor was still inadequate to support my four dependents and me, so I found part-time teaching at a community college to augment my salary and did various menial jobs whenever I could make time for them.

3   As Ramapo College grew, it hired extremely bright and mostly very nice young colleagues, but their concept of interdisciplinarity did not generally include psychohistory and was much narrower than mine. While lauding Ramapo's interdisciplinary approach, they also show a strong tendency to want to recreate aspects of their disciplinary graduate training.

4   Regrettably, the change in my title did not increase the frequency of my teaching explicitly psychohistorical courses.

5   Initially, a majority of the presenters at the first IPA conference in 1978 were academic historians; however, the cool to hostile reaction of their colleagues meant that the number of historians declined quickly and continued to decline. The total number of presenters also declined. Jacques Szaluta, "Psychohistorians Discuss Psychohistory: On the Third International Psychohistorical Association," *The Journal of Psychohistory*, Vol. 7 No. 3 (Winter 1979–80): p. 369, gives the decline of presenters from forty to thirty. In the contemporary IPA there are few historians who present, although 2016–2018 IPA President Ken Fuchsman is working hard to increase the numbers.

6   The best-known books condemning our field are as follows: Jacques Barzun, *Clio and the Doctors: History, Psycho-History and Quanto-History* (1974) and David E. Stannard, *Shrinking History: On Freud and the Failure of Psychohistory* (1980).

7   An example of popular anti-Freudianism occurred in my course on nineteenth-century Europe in which an older student referred to Freud as "Fraud" and denounced him in the strongest terms. In speaking privately, he told me that his daughter had serious psychological problems and that he felt defrauded by psychiatrists who he thought of as Freudians.

8 Lloyd deMause did block my assumption of the leadership of the IPA when I was vice president, but several years later I assumed the presidency. In about 2010, deMause's memory problems reached the point that his wife took over as publisher of the *Journal* and David Lotto became de facto editor.

9 Although Beisel has retired, his psychohistory course at SUNY-RCC continues to be taught by two colleagues, but without the same large enrollment.

10 When there was a major reorganization at Ramapo College, I proposed a four-year detailed psychohistory program to the school of business that their dean was excited about until he realized that psychologists would not accept it for credit.

11 George Kren was quite enthusiastic about the program, but he told me that Leon Rappoport and he could not get enough graduate students to make the program a success.

12 Paul H. Elovitz with David Cifelli, "Three Psychohistorical Journals," *Clio's Psyche*, Vol. 22 No. 1–2 (June–September 2015): pp. 74–80.

13 The official name was *The History of Childhood Quarterly: The Journal of Psychohistory* until 1976 when it officially became *The Journal of Psychohistory*.

14 Marshall Alcorn and Mark Bracher, two literature professors, started the group, which has very fruitful and lively meetings.

15 Lawrence J. Friedman and Peter Lawtner, who hosts the meetings in his home, are my source for this inadequately known group, which normally didn't refer to itself as psychohistorical, but does psychohistorical work. When the group met at the Harvard Club, graduate students who could not afford the dinners were allowed in for the lecture and discussion.

16 Cristian Tileagă and Jovan Byford, eds., *Psychology and History: Interdisciplinary Explorations* (Cambridge: Cambridge University Press, 2014): pp. 83–108.

17 Joan W. Scott, "The Incommensurability of Psychoanalysis and History," *History and Theory* (2012): pp. 40–63.

18 Boddice, "The Affective Turn: Historicising the Emotions," *History and Psychology* (2014): p. 149.

19 Boddice, "The Affective Turn," p. 148.

5

COMPARING THE EARLY FREUDIAN AND PSYCHOHISTORICAL MOVEMENTS

It is fruitful to compare and contrast the early Freudian and the psychohistorical movements. Clearly they are related, yet very different, in terms of acceptance, creativity, followership, leadership, openness to divergent ideas, originality, splitting, and other issues. I will start with a brief description of each of these important movements.

Sigmund Freud was such a creative and original thinker that people were drawn to him, and thus a movement was created. He also wrote beautiful German. First and foremost, Freud was a healer who enjoyed great success as a thinker as well. The international movement he started put pressure on him to act and react differently than as a healer and intellectual and brought out the more rigid side of his personality. Early biographers, such as Ernest Jones, depicted Freud as a heroic figure struggling against intense criticism and opposition. Most Freudian clinicians have followed in his footsteps, greatly appreciated their founder, and have had only a minor interest in his limitations. This was based, perhaps mostly, on their idealized transference to the originator of their field. In contrast, subsequent authors within and outside of the movement have written at length about Freud's limitations and weaknesses as a leader. Part of the unconscious and sometimes conscious motivations for this tendency to focus on Freud's leadership shortcomings are a process of de-idealization of the "good father," thus demonstrating one's independence from, or even hostility toward, him. A Freudian psychoanalyst friend wonders if I may be acting out my own Oedipal rebellion against Freud, Halpern, and deMause. Readers can come to their own conclusion.

How the early history of Freudianism relates to the organized psychohistorical movement is my primary concern. Clearly, there are many differences, but still significant similarities. One distinction is that leadership in the psychohistorical movement was never as focused on one individual as in Freudianism. Part of the reason for this was that psychohistory gradually came together over a period of time before becoming a somewhat organized entity in the 1970s.

Lloyd deMause admirably built a very successful automotive newsletter business in New York with impressive Broadway offices and about twenty-five full-time employees.[1] He was generally a very good organizer. Of course, psychohistorical articles and books appeared earlier, but only became a more cohesive and somewhat significant body of work in the 1950s and '60s with the publication of many valuable studies written by a variety of colleagues, including E.R. Dodds, Erik H. Erikson, Norman O. Brown, Alexander and Juliette George, and Robert Jay Lifton.[2]

Even when there was an enthusiastic, although small, group of supporters for psychohistory among academics, no one in psychohistory had anything like the authority of Sigmund Freud in the psychoanalytic movement. This helps to explain why the rivalries within it did not result in institutional splits. The founder of psychoanalysis could split with and ostracize Alfred Adler, Karl Jung, Otto Rank, Herbert Silberer, Victor Tausk, and others. In contrast, Lifton and Strozier might "bad mouth" deMause and those associated with the Institute for Psychohistory, *The Journal of Psychohistory*, and the IPA, but their control and influence was limited.[3] Lloyd deMause, the most controversial leader of psychohistory, sometimes offended colleagues with his editorial judgment, organizational decisions, and the extremity of his theories, but he did not exclude colleagues. In fact, he contained any disappointment he may have had when colleagues set up new organizations, such as the Psychohistory Forum (1982–) and the Group for the Psychohistorical Study of Film (1989–2008), and *Clio's Psyche* as a new publication.[4] On the other hand, he also encouraged a sense of "us" who have the truth of a scientific psychohistory and the courage to pursue it, versus those lacking in these attributes. As long as I felt a strong identification with deMause, as I did for about six or seven years, I was hesitant to go to ISPP meetings because they were "our rival."[5]

Psychohistory became a strong current in the 1970s, showing signs of acceptance by mainstream publications, although there were always very active naysayers. The prestigious *American Historical Review* (*AHR*), under Robert Webb (1968–1975) and to a lesser extent Otto Pflanze (1977–1985), was open to some explicitly psychohistorical articles, especially on Germany. The '70s were alive with both interest in and resistance to this new knowledge, and also struggling with how to institutionalize it. In this period, Lloyd deMause was working very hard to persuade psychoanalysts to focus on the history of childhood and beginning the process of building institutions through *The History of Childhood Quarterly: The Journal of Psychohistory* (1973), the Institute for Psychohistory (1975), the Psychohistory Press, the International Psychohistorical Association (IPA, 1977), and *The Journal of Psychoanalytic Anthropology* (1980–1987). The International Society for Political Psychology (ISPP) also had its inaugural meeting in Manhattan a week after the IPA. It created its own journal, *Political Psychology*, unlike the IPA, which had a newsletter. Despite the commonly held belief to the contrary, the IPA has no formal relationship with *The Journal of Psychohistory*.

Looking back at the early Freudians, the psychiatric institutions of Vienna and Europe were not eager to welcome Freud and his followers into their fold. Freud and his followers, in turn, developed their own institutions such as the International Psycho-Analytic Association and a large variety of training institutes. In my lifetime, a central issue has been the relationship of psychohistory to the existing disciplines. Academic psychologists, but not clinicians, overwhelmingly slammed their doors on those who were open to the new methodology. History departments were initially more ambivalent in their responses. In 1956, they were cool to William L. Langer of Harvard's call to the application of psychoanalysis to history as "the next assignment" for young historians in his American Historical Association Presidential Inaugural Address. However, some younger historians began to consider this approach, although they were very anxious and nervous to declare themselves to be practitioners of psychohistory. This was especially true of most members of American Historical Association's (AHA) Group for the Use of Psychology in History (GUPH).[6] They remained quite concerned about the reactions of the elders of history and uncertain about their relationship to the psychoanalytic clinicians they were reading and meeting. Their ambivalence was heightened by Erik Erikson's discomfort with the term "psychohistorian" and Robert Lifton changing the name of the Group for the Study of Psychohistorical Process, which he created with others in 1966, to simply Wellfleet. Wellfleet, the oldest psychohistorical group, met annually in the fall as an invitation-only seminar until Lifton ended it in 2015.

Lloyd deMause had the mentality of a businessman when it came to developing the field of psychohistory and *The Journal of Psychohistory*. He did not usually take rejection personally and continued to invite colleagues to write articles, serve on the editorial board of the very widely circulated *Journal*, and publish their work through his press. *Political Psychology*, the journal of the ISPP, came into existence in 1979 and continues to thrive, although it is not psychoanalytic in its approach. The *Psychohistory Review*,[7] which had an impressive group of academics on its editorial board, had built its subscription base to about 500 through word of mouth and colleagues requesting that their libraries subscribe to it. As mentioned above, the demise of the *Review* in 1999 was a serious loss to the field.[8]

While both psychoanalysis and psychohistory are intellectual disciplines, they differ in important respects. Psychohistory lacks the individual healing power of psychoanalysis, while the discipline created by Freud also provided a way of making a living; most of its adherents became therapists while psychohistory never provided an economic basis for adherents. This aspect has diminished the cohesion of the field. Furthermore, despite Freud's exaggeration of the enemies he faced, psychoanalysis was initially much more favorably received than psychohistory, which always had mixed reviews. Norman Kiell in 1988 published *Freud*

Without Hindsight: Reviews of his Work (1893–1939), revealing a far more positive reaction than one may gather from Jones and other early biographers.

To continue with comparisons, psychoanalysis was started by a Jew and his early followers were overwhelmingly Jewish, while psychohistory has always had a greater mixture of Jews (Gay, Lifton, Loewenberg, me, etc.) and gentiles (deMause, Langer, Strozier, Volkan, etc.) among its advocates, leaders, and prominent practitioners. I heard deMause speculate that if he were Jewish, he might be taken more seriously as an intellectual. However, very significantly, if we compare Freud with deMause, we find that both had a sense of specialness as young children; Amalia Freud called her son "my golden Sigi," and deMause spoke of having been the youngest child to read. Freud once saw himself as a conquistador of knowledge, and deMause viewed himself as a pathbreaker.

Clearly, both had issues with their fathers. Freud's elderly father disappointed him by not standing up to anti-Semites and being a poor provider. After his father's death when Sigmund was forty years old, he became intellectually most productive. This productivity is probably connected to his theory that the death of a father frees his son to reach his full potential. DeMause first appears to have taken his automotive executive father as his role model when his higher education began at Detroit's automotive college. Periodically, he expressed the fear that he would develop Alzheimer's as had his father, which tragically became a reality for him, as well as for his younger brother.

When deMause subsequently applied to Columbia for a liberal arts education and soon focused on child abuse, he was rejecting the father who had beaten him with a razor strap. I have no recollections of him speaking warmly about his father and virtually no memory at all of hearing about his mother.

Both men saw themselves as scientific, yet each had strong speculative inclinations, although Freud controlled these impulses better than deMause. Both leaders were inclined to have favorites, such as Adler and Jung for the Viennese and Henry Ebel, Glenn Davis, and Casper Schmidt for the American. The favorites of deMause were inclined to be brilliant and erratic, while Freud's generally seemed more grounded. With great insight, the founder of psychoanalysis recognized that "My emotional life has always insisted that I have an intimate friend and a hated enemy."[9] Such splitting was not unknown to the American, who spoke about splits being normal among groups. Though he had an "us vs. them" mentality regarding the Group for the Use of Psychology in History, he consciously sought to minimize splits within the IPA and Institute for Psychohistory.

Freud, born in the nineteenth century, could be tyrannical at times in dealing with his followers, while deMause could be unappreciative of the expectations and work of others and made abrupt changes as a leader, which alienated some of his followers. Some examples of this involve a contested IPA presidential election and then the termination of the Institute for Psychohistory's Saturday workshop meetings. At moments, his enthusiasm for something or somebody else caused him to be cut off from the emotional needs of individuals and other members of the group, as in the cases of Jacques Szaluta and me. Jacques Szaluta's incident involved the understanding of most early IPAers that the convention chair would then become president. Jacques, as convention chair, assumed he was set to succeed Dave Beisel as president. At lunch before the executive board meeting, Bernard Flicker impressed deMause with his good ideas for the organization, leading to deMause suggesting, "Why not have a contested IPA presidential election?" which then occurred and resulted in Flicker's election. Szaluta was understandably hurt and did not return to the organization for well over a decade, and even then only at my urging when we met at the ISPP and then the Forum. After Peter Petschauer did an excellent job of organizing the IPA's Washington conference in 1988, the only one not held in New York City, he was sharply criticized by deMause rather than praised. This led him to leave the organization for many years.

My incident was when he abruptly announced that he was ending the Saturday workshops of the Institute for Psychohistory that I had co-originated and then run myself for five years. When in 1982 his favorite, Casper Schmidt, planned large public psychohistorical meetings, he abruptly told me the small Work-In-Progress seminars would be ended. This was a totally unnecessary step because different audiences would be involved, but it probably had much to do with Schmidt's sense of "sibling rivalry" with me.[10] DeMause sometimes saw himself as the Freud of psychohistory and used the same initials (IPA) for the international movement he led in 1977 as Freud's much larger International Psychoanalytical Association created in 1910.

The Viennese wrote twenty-three volumes, while the New Yorker wrote seven. Freud was a meticulous scholar, although his historical materials were often far too speculative and therefore flawed. DeMause wrote copious footnotes for his "Evolution of Childhood," but they often don't specifically support what they are supposed to substantiate. Subsequently, he became much more careless in his scholarship as he assumed the role of the salesman for and "prophet of psychohistory." As my friend Sidney Halpern used to say about Marx, "while he was an incredibly acute student of capitalism, he then took on the role of prophet, acting as if what he expected to occur in 100 years had actually occurred." DeMause vacillated between being the realistic businessman and leader and the idealistic prophet, which resulted in many of his unfortunate decisions. David Beisel and I rolled our eyes at moments when we felt that the movement that deMause, so many others, and we had worked so hard to grow was once again being undercut.[11] The psychological term for this is "self-defeating," and of course Freud wrote about "Those Wrecked by Success." The inventor of psychoanalysis only had self-analysis, while the latter appeared to be in analysis throughout most of his adult life. Freud's brilliant originality inspired many, while deMause's originality has been much less impactful because most of his ideas are too extreme and unsubstantiated to be accepted by more than a few persons.

In choosing deMause for this comparison with Freud, I do not mean to argue that he was "the leader" of psychohistory, just the one who was organizationally most prominent. Naturally, I never worked with Freud; however, I worked closely with deMause in the early years and subsequently have maintained a cordial working relationship with few exceptions. He is the leader I can say the most about. In our period, Robert Jay Lifton was much better known and accepted in the intellectual community generally, but he did not involve himself in explicit psychohistorical organizations beyond the early Wellfleet group, and elsewhere his psychohistory was implicit, not explicit.[12] Vamık Volkan has had much greater international influence, but his approach is narrower than deMause's.

In retrospect, neither movement was able to ensconce itself within the academic departments in the U.S.A., although in Vienna as of 2005 there is a Sigmund Freud University teaching psychotherapy. The many institutes teaching psychoanalysis provide a solid base for continued support, while the future of psychohistory is much more precarious. Despite this academic resistance, both movements have had a profound impact on our thinking and offer great insights to individuals and society.[13] Both Freud and deMause focused on the importance of childhood, to which I will now turn.

Notes

1 David Beisel, who as editor of the *Journal* for nine years worked closely with deMause, reports that there were seven newsletters, including one for undertakers.

2 E.R. Dodds, *The Greeks and the Irrational* (1951); Erik H. Erikson, *Young Man Luther: A Study in Psychoanalysis and History* (1958); Norman O. Brown, *Life Against Death: The Psychoanalytical Meaning of History* (1959); Alexander and Juliette George, *Woodrow Wilson and Colonel House: A Personality Study* (1964); and Robert Jay Lifton, *Death in Life: Survivors of Hiroshima* (1968).

3 Robert Jay Lifton also badmouthed Vamık Volkan and his journal and center. I wondered if there was an underlying conscious or unconscious issue of rivalry because Volkan was also doing peacemaking as Lifton was doing at the Center for the Study of Violence and Human Survival.

4 When Bob Lentz and I started *Clio's Psyche* as a newsletter in 1994, deMause immediately asked me to make it the International Psychohistorical Association newsletter, which would have eliminated the need to raise money to support the publication. This did not fit my vision, and I immediately declined. The membership of the Psychohistory Forum has always supported its journal.

5 I found the ISPP to be an excellent organization, even though I was disappointed that psychohistory was only a small part of its activities.

6 Dick Schoewenwald (1927–1995) of Carnegie Mellon University was the founder of GUPH. Paul H. Elovitz, "In Memoriam: Richard L. Schoewenwald," *Clio's Psyche*, Vol. 2 No. 3 (December 1995): p. 72. See also, Paul H. Elovitz, "In Memoriam: H. Stuart Hughes (1916–1999): From the 'Supporting Cast' of Psychohistory," *Clio's Psyche*, Vol. 6 No. 3 (June 1999): p. 151.

7 Patrick Dunn is listed by *Gilmore, Comprehensive Bibliography*, p. ix as the founding editor of the *Psychohistory Review* when it started as a newsletter.

8 Paul H. Elovitz and David Cifelli, "Three Psychohistorical Journals," *Clio's Psyche*, Vol. 22 No. 1–2 (June–September 2015): pp. 74–80.

9 "The Interpretation of Dreams," *S.E.*, Vol. 5 (1900): p. 483.

10 As much as I prefer to be seen as a younger colleague of Lloyd rather than a disciple, there were some elements of discipleship at work. I complained to Sid Halpern about this deMausian tendency to seek disciples rather than colleagues.

11 While most IPAers trained as historians dropped out in frustration, David Beisel and I did not. Although he claimed to do archival research, in our time with deMause he never did archival research in the "dusty archives," despite his claim to the contrary.

12 Lifton's Center on Violence and Human Survival (1986–2002) did applied psychohistory, but without the name. Lifton headed it, but Strozier and his friend Michael Flynn, who tragically died very young, seemed to do most of the work.

13 A version of this chapter first appeared as the article, "A Comparison of Early Freudianism with the Psychohistorical Movement," *Clio's Psyche*, Vol. 22, No. 1–2 (June–September 2015): pp. 20–25.

6

A PSYCHOHISTORIAN'S APPROACH TO CHILDHOOD AND CHILDREARING

William Wordsworth long ago recognized that "the child is the father of the man" because childhood is when we form our personalities.[1] How each of us was raised and how we see our first life experiences ultimately influences how we view childhood and raise our own children. The emphasis of psychoanalysis on the importance of early childhood is what led many clinicians and scholars to psychohistory. Indeed, the focus on childhood and its history is integral to psychohistory and one of its great strengths. Lloyd deMause's early focus on it was crucial to his attraction as a leader of psychohistory, as reflected in his initially naming his journal *The History of Childhood Quarterly: The Journal of Psychohistory*. Childhood, specifically the formative years of world and cultural leaders, comes up repeatedly in many psychohistorical works, not just psychobiographies.

This chapter is mostly a discussion of childhood in contemporary America, with historical comparisons. It is also partly a memoir of my own childhood, parenting three boys and a girl, teaching young people for over half a century, and practicing as a child therapist for two decades. It is tempting to take either an optimistic or pessimistic position regarding the condition of children in modern America. Let me start with the optimistic viewpoint.

Never in history have most American children had such a high standard of living, so much personal space, such rich food, so much disposable income, such technological wonders, so many rights, and so many laws to protect them from abuse at home, school, and work. Wealth is lavished on our children. More than the gross national product of most countries is spent on schooling and the transportation costs involved. Suburban parents often organize their lives around chauffeuring their children to activities, such as Boy or Girl Scouts, dance, martial arts, music, and sports, designed to enrich their development. Vacations often mean that the kids get to travel to Disney World and other exciting locations in sunny climates.

In modern middle class society, children are loved and invested in as never before. Throughout history when many children, and often their mothers in childbirth, died young, the emotional and financial investment of parents in their children was much more limited than it is today when practically all newborns survive. As suburban children reach adolescence, parental concern is increasingly about higher education. The first college choices of senior high school students who can afford financially and emotionally to be away from home are likely to be where their friends are interested in attending or are often close to the beach, good skiing, mountain sports, party towns, or other recreational dreams. I often wonder if there has ever been such a group of self-sacrificing parents as we have at the present time. The hard work and self-sacrificing parenting ideal is perhaps one reason that so many young Americans are hesitant to bring the next generation into our world.

A young mother tells me that there is competition among parents to reach unrealistic ideals. Many paint a picture of perfect childrearing and a perfect life on Facebook, to which others then compare themselves to. Pinterest (another social media site with a strong appeal to American women on the Internet) is all about sharing ideas. It sets up an impossible ideal of continually occupying children with enriching activities and perfectly crafted meals. There is constantly a stream of contradictory advice, such as letting your children play outside, but with sun protection, but not the chemical-filled sunscreen. "Let them play independently, but make sure they socialize, and make sure they are kind to the other children, but don't force them to share." It goes on and on, worrying parents.

The optimistic position on the state of children is further strengthened by comparing the lives of twenty-first-century American children with those of earlier periods in history and in the less developed world of today. Baby boys are not sacrificed at birth by their parents to propitiate the gods.[2] Babies born without male genitalia no longer run a risk of infanticide on the basis of being "another worthless girl." The infanticide extant in America today is usually that of the desperate, drug addicted, insane, or terrorized. Rather than say, like the ancient philosopher Aristippus, that a man can toss away his newborns as he did his spit or lice, even deformed infants are cared for in our society. In the ancient world the deformed were almost automatically killed. In American society, even the interests of the unborn are heartily defended—though ironically often by the very same people who advocate the execution of adults.

Children today are not sent off to wet nurses, as they were so commonly throughout history, for the sake of preserving their mothers' shapely breasts and the pleasures of the husbands. Infants are no longer swaddled to keep them under control. Children are not forced to serve "their betters" or executed for the disloyalty of their parents, as happened to the children of nobles sent as hostages to the lord's court. The kissing and fondling of the nipples and private parts of children, which was quite common in the age of Louis XIII of France, is no longer socially sanctioned.[3] Indeed, such behavior is considered sexual abuse, and teachers, doctors, and other professionals are required to report possible cases of any abuse. In contrast to the nineteenth century, and despite the efforts of some religious fundamentalists, children are raised to believe that their bodies are their own. Their hands or genitals will not fall off if they engage in masturbation or sex without the benefit of clergy. Girls are not legally subject to arranged marriages, as was my grandmother in Poland and as children still are in parts of the world, but have choices regarding marriage and so much else in their lives. Contemporary children are not heavily beaten, placed in stocks, and put to work at ages that stunt their growth. If one wants to know the extent of the abuse and suffering of children in history, one need only look at Lloyd deMause's pathbreaking essay.[4]

The opportunities available to children in the U.S. and Western Europe are amazing in comparison to the limited choices of youngsters in the past and even in the underdeveloped world today. This is why there is such a flood of immigrants eager to come to these places legally or illegally. I could write at great length about these historical and developed versus less developed world comparisons, but I think the essential point has been made. Instead, I will turn to my own life story with the focus on childrearing—recalling and analyzing my own story not just years ago, but repeatedly over time and created the model by which I, like other psychohistorians, have come to understand the lives of the persons we study. Again, the importance of childhood is not only to the child, but to the society that child is a part of.

As the third child and second son of striving, hard-working Jewish immigrant parents from Eastern Europe, who fled the ravages of war and the poverty it brought, my childhood was centered on "my father's store."[5] Dad was a self-taught, highly skilled furrier who started his own business in Bridgeport, Connecticut during the Great Depression after he was blacklisted in New York City for being a part-time union organizer. There was love, but my parents were very busy people who didn't have nearly as much time for their children as they would have liked. Childrearing was overwhelmingly Mom's responsibility, although she worked the same long hours as Dad and did the household tasks. I was a premature baby cared for by my paternal grandmother for the first few years of my life, which I have no memory of, followed by living over my father's store in a dangerous neighborhood until we moved when I was six. There were some intrusive parenting elements in my childhood, especially the enemas I so dreaded. Because Mom was always multitasking, a way of getting close to her was to be her helper. I was proud when I could take over my brother's job of sweeping and helping in the store—even though it resulted in lots of criticism if I raised dust as I swept. For a year I lost my helper's job to a severely traumatized Holocaust survivor who was promised employment for a year as a way of his coming to America from a displaced persons camp in Germany.

Dad was my hero for a number of reasons. When at age five I was dying of an undiagnosed ruptured appendix, he insisted on taking me to the hospital. I still have scars to remind me that, in about the same time period, he came to my rescue as I played alone in the backyard when, in trying to see my one occasional playmate, I managed to hang myself on a fence by the skin of my throat and another time had a very large, deep cut in my arm. I was intrigued by his adventures as a boy in Europe in a time of war and revolution. I was needy, but quite compliant and very proud that he never hit me, as opposed to my older brother who was much more assertive and independent. My mother once slapped me hard on the chest when I was about thirteen or fourteen after I provoked her. Despite being the baby of the family, often looked after by my slightly older sister, I still had to do many things on my own that modern children don't have to do, like walking to school, taking the city bus at an early age, and making my own lunch. Life centered on the store and school. After a slow start, I became a good, college-bound student. My father, like so many other Jewish immigrants, hoped I would become a medical doctor with, in his words, "a cash register." My idealistic mother dreamed I would become a college professor. When away in college and then the Army, I rebelled, disappointing both parents.[6]

My first wife and I married and had children when we were quite young. We did not know each other or ourselves very well and had very unrealistic fantasies about what living together would entail. We were both virgins when we married. As a father, I loved having children and never hit them; however, I was so busy getting a doctoral degree, furthering my career, and working part time jobs to make ends meet that I have always regretted not spending more time with them in their earliest years.[7] As the youngest of three children, I was troubled by my eldest son's sense of entitlement vis-à-vis his younger siblings, which mirrored my brother's attitude.

My marriage was soon in trouble. While tension between my spouse and me grew, I worked extremely hard and tried to ignore our marital estrangement; after all, my parents' marriage had been quite rocky at times. However, divorce was becoming a much more acceptable option for women and society in the 1970s, but not for me; it was extremely important for me to stay married and not be separated from my children. A Catholic friend insisted that I was a much better Catholic than he was, especially when it came to divorce and issues of conscience. However, eventually, I accepted a trial separation, during the early period of which I was seeing my kids four times a week—given the tension coming from their parents this was far too much for them. I discovered I was much happier living apart from my wife, and I soon met the very different type of woman whom I eventually married.[8] Helping to raise my second wife's son was a revelation to me because he was so very different and more outspoken than my own children. The divorce was hard on the children, who have had good lives and relationships with both parents, yet I must agree with Judith Wallenstein that there is a lifelong impact. It should be borne in mind that from a historical perspective, divorce is not nearly as damaging as parental loss through death, so often at childbirth, which was commonplace in history.

Why does this all matter? I've learned from my own story how, in our society, many youngsters suffer the disruption of their lives and sometimes the loss of their parents through divorce. Some authorities argue that divorce is no more, or even less, developmentally harmful than growing up in bad relationships.[9] A pessimist about the situation of children in America might argue that we give children the best of everything, except for what really counts: a consistent, secure, loving environment and clear parental role models. Children in history learned by watching and doing, usually with one-on-one instruction by parents or the master to whom they were apprenticed, rather than by being forced into schools, as in our society.[10] I sometimes feel that, psychologically, children have never had a more difficult time growing up than in our modern world, partly because of the uncertainties and ambivalences of their parents who so often do not even stay married "for the sake of the children," which was much more likely the case with earlier generations.[11]

What is happening now is also food for psychohistorical thought. Today, growing up is bewildering because children are given mixed messages. Children are raised in a culture of fear, engendered by anxieties spread on the Internet, radio, television, and in the newspapers, giving them the impression that the aberrant behavior of deviants in any part of the world is about to endanger them. Thus the sense of basic trust has diminished dramatically in our society.[12] For example, in listening to the media, children could easily form the impression that every priest is a child molester or that every policeman shoots blacks.

Contemporary parents are often confused and guilt-ridden as to how they should raise and discipline their children. Consequently, many seek to "buy them off," providing them with the "things" that children are convinced by television are necessary to "survive" within their social group. They are often awed by the experts and fail to trust their own better parenting impulses. Consistency in children's schedules has become a casualty to the modern hectic lifestyle. The entire family eating dinner together every night has ceased to be an ideal for many families as parents work longer hours and chauffeur their kids to sports, clubs, friends, and part-time work. The lead article of a recent Sunday news magazine proclaimed that one of every five teenagers had seriously considered terminating their own lives, proving how suicidal thoughts run rampant today.[13] Teenagers are clearly confused and sometimes tempted by suicide in a society geared to instant gratification: where you just click the channel to change the fantasy you want to pursue. Frustration in life is inevitable and there is less preparation for it in our society.

Children are unconsciously, and sometimes consciously, quite sensitive to the disclaimed feelings of their parents, which they may act out. When I taught at Temple University, my first wife was quite nervous and unconsciously angry that the owner of the house we rented was coming to inspect her property. Our three-year-old son, normally a quite well behaved child, climbed on a chair and then the stove and countertops while this woman was checking her property. In doing child, adolescent, and family therapy, I observed many instances of this acting-out phenomenon.

The healthy emotional growth of children is impeded by role reversals that are more common in fragmented families where a parent becomes more emotionally dependent on the children than where there is a consistent parental partner. I recollect an example of this from an early child therapy case. A very bright six-year-old of professional parents was inclined to act out. The problem was that the divorcing parents were unconsciously treating him like the adult in the family. The crucial break-through came when the parents reluctantly had to confront their role reversal and the fact that no matter how bright a child is, he still has the emotional needs of a child. The family did much better after they incorporated this knowledge into their parenting. They left their son free to be a child again.

Another family brought in their twelve-year-old son for treatment because he was beginning to follow in the path of his seven-years-older brother, who had dropped out of school and gotten into trouble to the point where the parents had "kicked him out of our home" for his alcoholic disruption of their lives and poor example for his younger siblings. My patient was doing poorly in school and misbehaving at home. In fact, this lively boy was beginning to act out the family's denied and repressed anger. His father had been severely depressed, but functional as a professional, since returning from military service in Vietnam. His mother was furious at her husband for his prolonged depression but "too nice" to openly express her anger toward her husband or even her sons. The eldest son was unconsciously delegated the role of expressing anger and being the family lightning rod for the discontent of others. When the older brother left home—establishing a productive life—the pressure was then unconsciously placed on his younger brother to follow in the same self-destructive teenage pattern. Therapy helped the family find a more positive path for their younger son.

As this family's story shows, the work that psychoanalysts do gives them a window into the impact of history on the psyche of the young. It is only natural then that some analysts have gravitated toward psychohistory; we deal with the microcosm in our consulting rooms and then question how millions of others have been similarly affected.

Security is one of the most basic needs of childhood. Insecurity was the norm in America even before the September 11 attack. A student reports that there are now twenty-five security guards working in the suburban high school of about 1,000 students from which she graduated from a few years ago. The guards are trying to enforce a moderate level of safety and maintain some level of tranquility within this multiracial school not far from New York City.

Childhood is such a confused time for many people that they are reluctant to bring others into the world. Unprecedented numbers of the middle class are no longer even having children, while those who do are much less inclined to get married. Most population growth in the U.S. actually comes from the larger families of immigrants, who are more optimistic about bringing new life into the world as they enter a society with a higher standard of living than the one from which they came.

In setting up a dichotomy between optimists and pessimists on the condition of children in our society, I am articulating contradictory thoughts and feelings I have heard from others on the subject. Some of these I share. Something I am not ambivalent about is the value of having children for both individuals and society. I commonly say that the most fulfilling thing we as human beings do is to have children. The next thing I then say is that the most difficult and challenging experience of life is parenting.[14] Other parents tend to respond with a comment or look of agreement, while those who have never had children are inclined to give me a thoughtful, uncertain, almost worried look.

We urge our daughters to get a good education, often to the level of doctoral degrees, and then to become established in their professions. While this is happening, their biological clocks are running, but often their boyfriends are even shier about going to the altar than many of them. Forty percent of U.S. babies today are born to unwed mothers, although sometimes with the father being present.[15] There are certainly a lot of women who worry about missing out on the joys of parenting and doing for the next generation what was done for them, however imperfectly. If they are fortunate enough to have children, they face the unique opportunities and difficulties of parenting in our society.

Raising children is a challenge for all parents, including full-time mothers and homemakers with the support of loving husbands with a good income. Fewer mothers I know have this support system and that of parents and siblings who lend a helping hand in emergencies. Modern professional women in our society struggle with these issues as never before.[16]

This chapter has been mostly about children in middle class, suburban America. Of course, there are many other Americas. There are the kids of the African-American ghettos, the children of the urban immigrants, those of the small towns and of the big cities where there is still public transportation. I think of how emotionally difficult life is for children whose parents immigrate to the U.S. while leaving the children behind in the care of grandmothers and other relatives. Other children come to mind, including my African-born honor student who speaks four languages, is from a polygamous family, and had a personal crisis when she reluctantly confided to me that her "aunt died because of a voodoo curse." I am reminded of my orthodox Jewish student who graduated college the month she turned twenty with high honors and awards, despite her parents pressuring her for several years to enter an arranged marriage. She had exercised her right of refusal of the marriage arrangements to the point that she feared the negative reactions of her parents and community. In addition, she felt left out because her same-age girlfriends all had several babies and she was not even married. There are certainly many Americas not dealt with in this brief, impressionistic discussion.[17]

The optimists and pessimists regarding the condition of children in modern America each make many worthwhile points. Children are both better and worse off in our society, depending upon which group of them we study and what aspects of their lives are examined. They also are different because they grew up under very dissimilar conditions than did their parents and ancestors. My childhood, education, and study of childhood influenced how I raised my children. Parental expectations of my society have changed dramatically, but the attachment of parent and child remains quite strong. I will next discuss prominent psychohistorians, focusing partly on their childhoods when possible.

Notes

1 William Wordsworth, "My Heart Leaps Up When I Behold," in Edward Dowden, ed., *Poems by William Wordsworth* (New York: Ginn & Company, 1898).

2 Lloyd deMause, *The History of Childhood* (New York: Psychohistory Press, 1974), pp. 25–32.

3 Elizabeth W. Marvick, *Louis XIII: The Making of a King* (1986). *The Young Richelieu: A Psychoanalytic Approach to Leadership* (1983) is another fine study by Marvick.

4 "The Evolution of Childhood," *The History of Childhood Quarterly: The Journal of Psychohistory*, Vol. 1 (1974): p. 536ff.

5 The reference to "my father's store" reflects the chauvinism of the period. My mother may not have known how to drive a car or do the finest craftsmanship required to create expensive coats, but she was absolutely a central part of the business because of her skills as a salesperson, seamstress, organizer, and accountant. Quite importantly, Mom could read and write English while Dad, who had almost no formal schooling, could write little more than his name.

6 Regrettably, it was only a few years after my mother's early death from cancer that I settled on becoming a college professor.

7 Before becoming small capitalists, both my parents were left wing organizers. While my primary motivation in cleaning offices, delivering bakery products, beer, and later milk, driving trucks, working in warehouses, and so forth was economic, there was also an element of identification with their youthful values.

8 An important reason why my first marriage floundered was that both my first wife and I were not good at directly expressing our needs to each other. My second wife is much more outspoken, which has been a good thing for our relationship.

9 E. Mavis Hetherington and John Kelly, *For Better or for Worse: Divorce Reconsidered* (2002).

10 Of course, masters could be abusive to their apprentices. For example, the future great British engineer Thomas Telford's (1757–1834) widowed mother was sure his career was ruined when as a fourteen-year-old he ran away from his stonemason master who beat her son "without reason."

11 A quarter century of studies of 131 children of divorced parents by Dr. Judith Wallerstein have argued that the detrimental effects of divorce are lifelong. J. S. Wallerstein, J. M. Lewis and S. Blakeslee, *The Unexpected Legacy of Divorce* (2000); S. R. Rappaport, "Deconstructing the Impact of Divorce on Children," *Family Law Quarterly*, Vol. 47 No. 3 (2013): pp. 353–377; Clorinda Vélez, S. A. Wolchik, J-N. Tein and I. Sandler, "Protecting Children From the Consequences of Divorce: A Longitudinal Study of the Effects of Parenting on Children's Coping Processes," *Child Development*, Vol. 82 No. 1 (2011): pp. 244–257.

12 "Trust in America, a Six-Part Series, 28 January–4 February 1996," *Washington Post*; Kostendin Kushlev and Jason Proulx, "The Social Costs of Ubiquitous Information: Consuming Information on Mobile Phones Is Associated with Lower Trust," *Plos ONE*, Vol. 11 No. 9 (2016): pp. 1–8.

13 Dianne Hales and Robert Hales, "When a Teenager Is Sad," *Parade Magazine* (5 May 2002); Frédéric N. Brière, P. Rohde, J. R. Seeley, D. Klein and P. M. Lewinsohn, "Adolescent Suicide Attempts and Adult Adjustments," *Depression and Anxiety*, Vol. 32 No. 4 (April 2015): pp. 270–276.

14 This is especially true when I had the impulse to say the same thing to my children that my parents did and about which I swore as a teenager that I would never say.

15 "Unmarried Childbearing," *Centers for Disease Control and Prevention* (31 March 2017), Web, 27 June 2017. www.cdc.gov/nchs/fastats/unmarried-childbearing.htm.

16 Sylvia Ann Hewlett, *Creating a Life: Professional Women and the Quest for Children* (2002); Anita M. Harris, *Broken Patterns: Professional Women and the Quest for a New Feminine Identity* (2014).

17 An early version of this article appeared as one of fourteen articles in *Clio's Psyche* in a special issue on childhood. It was in Vol. 9 No. 1 (June 2002): pp. 1–6.

7

PROMINENT PSYCHOHISTORIANS LIFTON, DEMAUSE, AND VOLKAN

Applied psychoanalysis, political psychology, and psychobiography, subsumed under the category of psychohistory, have had many hundreds of significant contributors for over a century. Robert Jay Lifton (1926–), Lloyd deMause (1931–), and Vamık Volkan (1932–) are three leaders of the field and advocates of peace. While having much in common, they each have very different achievements, approaches, goals, and impacts on the development of contemporary psychohistory. My focus is on how their backgrounds, life experiences, and personalities influenced their scholarly work and role in psychohistory. Each will be discussed and then compared, contrasted, and assessed. The long-term prospects for the continued influence of their ideas and the institutions they built will be examined to measure the legacy they will leave in psychohistory.

Robert Jay Lifton is a scholar, activist, and pioneering psychohistorian. He was born to a Jewish businessman and his wife in Brooklyn, New York in 1926 and educated in the city. Robert attended Cornell University, medical school at New York Medical College, and then trained as a psychiatrist. He reports that his best psychiatric teachers were psychoanalysts, but he was always ambivalent about analysis. He lauded it as a great intellectual breakthrough, but also compared it to the totalism of Chinese thought reform. Lifton trained as an analyst for two years before he dropped out of the analytic institute to return to the Far East for research. The Nazis, World War II, and violence generally are central to his consciousness. Yale University hired this bright young psychiatrist, but first he had to fulfill military service that would change the direction of his life. He accepted a commission in the Air Force, where he could function as a psychiatrist, rather than allowing himself to be drafted as a private in the Army. His work in Japan and Korea, evaluating brainwashed former prisoners of war of the Chinese Communists, fascinated him and led to studies of priests and others subjected to "thought reform."[1]

Erik Erikson's focus on identity became central to Lifton's thinking. He reports being "spellbound" by this mentor and friend, and he prides himself on carrying on Erikson's work. At Lifton's summer home in Wellfleet on Cape Cod with Erikson, Bruce Mazlish, and others, he formed the oldest continuous psychohistory group, which functioned from 1966 to 2015, mostly meeting for three-day seminars every fall.[2] By comparison, the International Psychohistorical Association (IPA) and the International Society for Political Psychology (ISPP) began meeting twelve years later. For three years, Lifton's meeting was labeled the Group for the Study of Psychohistorical Process, but the name was later shortened to the Wellfleet Meetings. The American Academy of Arts and Sciences, the sponsor of the early meetings, wanted the "Wellfleetians" to create an academic discipline of psychohistory and eventually become a training center for it. Lifton writes that the participants soon gave up this "illusion" in favor of informal, more imaginative, freewheeling meetings with little structure. Like Erikson, Lifton considers himself to be a psychohistorian, but does not like to use the word as a noun. After the early "illusion" period, Lifton shifted his view and opposed creating a separate field of psychohistory.

Lifton received various grants, including a "five-year dream grant" to support his brainwashing and totalism work, and Yale University was quite tolerant of his delays in taking up his duties in New Haven.[3] It should be pointed out that Lifton has received a remarkable amount of financial and other support throughout his career, which has allowed him to be a perpetual psychohistorical student of brainwashing, the impact of the first nuclear bomb on the survivors of Hiroshima, the trauma of war on veterans of Vietnam, the evil of Nazi doctors, the Aum Shinrikyo subway bombing cult, millennialism, and much more.[4] His quest has been to determine how humans struggle to live "in the face of death." He has been an anti-nuclear and anti-war activist as well as a scholar. In keeping with Eriksonian disciplined subjectivity, he attained extraordinary insight by intertwining his own personal subjective experience with his scholarly narrative.[5]

This dual drive of the scholar/activist led him to leave his Sterling Professorship at Yale to found and head The Center for the Study of Violence and Human Survival at John Jay College of the City University of New York (CUNY) from 1985–2003. At the Center, peacemakers from the United Nations, scholars, and many others met with therapists, historians, political scientists, and psychologists to deepen their understanding of the difficult problems they faced. Eventually, when Lifton's financial support was cut by CUNY, he retired. His younger colleague, the historian/psychoanalyst Charles Strozier (1946–), transformed the Violence Center into the Center on Terrorism to help police and firefighters-in-training develop a psychosocial approach to their work. Since then Lifton has had honorary professorships, including at Harvard.

Lloyd deMause is a psychohistorical organizer, meta-theorist, and visionary. Born in 1931 in Michigan as the elder of two sons of an auto executive, he was a precocious child and eventually graduated from an automotive college in

Michigan. In the era of a draft, he served as an enlisted man in the Army during the Korean War. He wondered about all the abandoned children sleeping under bridges in Korea, and this experience led to thinking more about childhood. Subsequent to his military service, he became interested in the liberal arts, studying at Columbia University in New York City, prior to working on a graduate degree in political science there. However, administrator Herbert Dean at the school refused him permission to write an explicitly psychoanalytic doctoral dissertation. Unlike some others with similar interests who wrote camouflaged psychoanalytically informed dissertations without top administrative approval, deMause quit graduate school and went back into the business world. There, he built a sound financial basis for his psychohistorical goals by creating a company that published newsletters for the automotive industry. The Saturday Workshop meetings of the Institute for Psychohistory were held in the elegant New York conference room of his Atcom Publishing Company on Broadway, not many blocks from his apartment on Riverside Drive, where he spent as much time as possible raising his first son in what he called "helping mode parenting." He is passionate about improving the life of children, convinced that children raised in the helping mode will be more peaceful and much better human beings.

Lloyd deMause trained at a psychoanalytic institute for a few years without seeing any patients because he wanted to analyze Hitler, not living patients, and worked for a while within the psychoanalytic community on issues of childrearing. However, he became frustrated by the slow progress he was making, and in the early 1970s, deMause began to build psychohistory institutions. He started the Institute for Psychohistory, *The Journal of Psychohistory* (originally named *The History of Childhood*), the Psychohistory Press, and the International Psychohistorical Association (IPA). He edited and wrote various psychohistorical books.[6] He sees himself as a scholar and a "meta-theorist" of social theory, propounding a scientific psychohistory. "The Evolution of Childhood" (1974) is his work that has had the greatest impact on psychoanalytically inclined historians like this author. His fantasy analysis methodology offers insights into national fantasies and other large-group behaviors. In many respects he assumed the role of a prophet of psychohistory, which inspired some, but turned off others, especially after they examined the weaknesses in his scholarship. The extremity of his views on fantasy analysis, the fetal origins of history, and social alters led to many colleagues shunning him and refusing to have anything to do with him or those who were perceived as close to him.

More positively, *The Journal of Psychohistory* is the only profitable journal in the field, which is quite an accomplishment because scholarly journals normally need the financial backing of universities or foundations. At one point he reported that it had eight thousand subscribers, although at the present time it is well below a thousand. More than anything else, deMause deserves credit for bringing many likeminded colleagues together around his journal and the IPA to develop the psychohistorical paradigm.

Vamık Volkan is a peacemaker, theorist, and the leading exemplar of applied psychohistory. Born into a Turkish family of educators on British Cyprus, Vamık learned about ethnic identity and conflict as he grew up on an island divided between Greeks and a Turkish minority. He subsequently went to the capital of Turkey for his medical training, and at age twenty-five the young physician emigrated to the U.S. and became a citizen. Here, he trained as a psychoanalyst, practiced psychiatry, and worked as the medical administrator of the University of Virginia's Blue Ridge Hospital from 1978 to 1994. Meanwhile, in the 1960s and '70s, Cyprus exploded in violence between the Greeks and the Turkish minority, causing him great concern and survivor's guilt because he lived in the safety of America.

His third profession as a psychoanalytic political psychologist was unexpected. After Anwar Sadat of Egypt amazed the world in 1977 by flying to Israel and telling the Knesset that seventy percent of the problem between Arabs and Israelis was psychological, Volkan stepped into the role of becoming a peacemaker. When the Committee on Psychiatry and Foreign Affairs of the American Psychiatric Association started to arrange unofficial meetings between Egyptians and Israelis, and eventually Palestinians, he joined the effort. He was one of the founders of the International Society for Political Psychology (ISPP) in 1978 and was its fourth president. At the University of Virginia, he established the interdisciplinary Center for the Study of Mind and Human Interaction (1987–2003), which focused on such issues as ethnic tensions, leader-follower relationships, national identity, racism, societal trauma, and the transgenerational transmissions of identity and trauma. Shortly after, he started the journal *Mind and Human Interaction: Windows Between History, Culture, Politics, and Psychoanalysis* (1989–2005), which was devoted to the same issues.

With a large network of international colleagues, Dr. Volkan has worked in over a dozen countries in Eastern Europe and Western Asia. From 1989 to 1998, he was a member of the International Negotiation Network under the chairmanship of former President Carter. In 2008, Volkan started the International Dialogue Initiative (IDI), which he leads along with Israeli psychologist Robi Friedman, British psychiatrist/politician Lord John Alderdice, and Gerard Fromm of Yale University. For years it was organized out of the Austen Riggs Center in Stockbridge, Massachusetts, where he served from 2003–2013 as the senior scholar at the Erikson Institute for Education and Research when not on his extensive travels.

This energetic man has had a remarkable number of visiting professorships and awards. He has authored, co-authored, or edited about sixty books, published in a variety of languages. Some are comprised of case studies describing and explaining his major concepts in the context of his work defusing hatreds that could lead to violence. His concepts of chosen traumas and chosen glories focus on how the identities of ethnic and national groups are shaped by shared suffering and triumph. He has developed the concept of time collapse, which explains how a group can focus on a trauma occurring hundreds of years before and speak as though it were a recent occurrence. An example of this is how, during the bloody struggles in the former Yugoslavia, Serbian leaders spoke of their defeat in the Battle of Kosovo of 1389 as a justification for their genocidal actions against Muslims. Volkan writes of entitlement ideologies that justify aggressive behavior on the basis of past history or suffering. He explains how linking objects, which may be no more than a pebble or a parakeet, are symbols connecting individuals to their ethnic or national group in times of stress.

A comparison of these three major leaders of psychohistory is in order. All (as of May 2018) are now in advanced age, with Lifton being the oldest at age ninety-two, deMause at eighty-six, and Volkan the youngest at eighty-five. They were born respectively into Jewish, Protestant, and Muslim families. Each is the eldest son, Lifton with an older sister, deMause the elder of two sons, and Volkan with two older sisters. They were born in Brooklyn, Detroit, and British Cyprus. The fathers of the first two were middle class businessmen, and the Cypriot comes from a family of educators. All three showed signs of specialness. The two American-born colleagues showed signs of promise in their achievement: Lifton graduated high school at age 16, Cornell two years later, and after two years in medical school was on to his residency. DeMause was pictured at age two as the youngest reader in a Ripley's "Believe It or Not" news clip and was intensively trained as a child to be a concert pianist. Volkan reports being a "replacement child" for a distinguished and wealthy maternal great-grandfather in Ottoman Turkey prior to the British taking over Cyprus in 1878. This contributed to a sense of importance and the need to make a difference in the world.

In terms of military experience, a general requirement for American men of their era, Lifton served as an Air Force psychiatrist and deMause as an enlisted soldier. The experiences they both had serving in Korea influenced their subsequent research. Their colleague born in Cyprus was not required to do military service.

Volkan not only fully embraced psychoanalysis as a practitioner and supervisor, but also sought to apply it to large-group identity and peacemaking. While Lifton and deMause had some psychoanalytic training and were quite influenced by its concepts, they didn't practice as analysts. Lifton saw it as a type of totalism that he disdained, while deMause's interests were focused elsewhere with analysis always being basic to his thinking. All three individuals created institutions to perpetuate their ideas: Wellfleet and the Center for the Study of Violence and Human Survival for Lifton; the Institute for Psychohistory, the International Psychohistorical Association, and *The Journal of Psychohistory* for deMause; and the Center for the Study of Mind and Human Interaction with its journal *Mind and Human Interaction* and the International Dialogue Initiative for Volkan.

Personal experiences undoubtedly influenced each of their lives and work. Being beaten by an authoritarian father with a razor strap left deMause determined to understand and combat child abuse. Volkan felt survivor's guilt when living in the safety of America while his family suffered in his turbulent homeland.

Lifton, as a Jew in the era of Hitler and the Holocaust, also felt some guilt at his comparative safety.

Professionally, Lifton has had distinguished professorships at Yale and the City University of New York based upon his much-lauded work as a psychiatric researcher, scholar, author, and public intellectual. Volkan's career has also been in academia at the University of Virginia as a hospital administrator, professor, and psychiatrist. These two have been well funded for their work, compared to most academics, by academia, foundations, and the government. In contrast, deMause created a successful publishing business so he could spend his time on psychohistorical scholarship and organizing. He never had an academic appointment, although he taught adjunct classes for a few years and gave some lectures at universities.

All three are theoretical innovators: Lloyd deMause developed the concepts of the evolution of childrearing (based on his psychogenetic theory), fantasy analysis, the fetal origins of history, helping mode parenting, poison containers, poisonous placentas, and social alters; Vamık Volkan developed a methodology of dialogues between enemies and concepts including accordion phenomenon, chosen glories, chosen traumas, entitlement ideologies, ethnic tents, hot spots, linking objects, and time collapse; and Robert Lifton developed an interview methodology and the concepts of doubling, the protean self, psychic numbing, and totalism. Volkan's dialogue among enemies, Lifton's interview methodologies, and, to a lesser extent, deMause's focus on historical childrearing are influential.

Public recognition for Lifton includes a National Book Award, Nobel Lectureship, Holocaust Memorial Award, and the Gandhi Peace Award. Volkan is the recipient of numerous awards, including the Sigmund Freud Award given by the city of Vienna. He was nominated four times for a Nobel Peace Prize with letters from twenty-seven countries. In contrast, awards have eluded deMause, who has worked outside of academia.

Now to their analysis, the continuity of their work, and my conclusion. Each of these talented men has found a unique career path, not following the typical academic track of the teacher and scholar. Their teaching has been focused on colleagues and others rather than young students. All three have won acclaim within divergent circles but have also been subject to criticism. In his remarkable career as an activist, public intellectual, and scholar, Lifton has faced criticism. To some, it was improper for a distinguished professor to spend a night in jail because of his anti-nuclear activism. David Beisel suggested that one of the reasons Lifton came up with the concepts of doubling and numbing is that he did not want to use the psychoanalytic terms of splitting, dissociation, and repression to describe similar phenomena. Colleagues who are explicit advocates of psychohistory and political psychology have seen him holding back the progress of the field by, at least in his early days, condemning those—this author included—who wrote psychobiographies of presidential candidates and downplaying his identification as a psychohistorian, while shunning others in the field as being too extreme and even "cultist."

Reactions to deMause, the most productive psychohistorical organizer and institution builder, have prevented his theories from gaining a wider following. His ideas about fantasy analysis, the fetal origins of history, poisonous placentas and mothers, and social alters are simply too extreme for most academics and clinicians who see them as speculative and reductionist. When he introduced them at the Institute for Psychohistory Workshops that I chaired or at the IPA, he often said something like, "This will shock you and you will think it is crazy, but my research shows that. . . ." I found them to be interesting, but unproven, and in some cases, such as the fetal origins of history, virtually unprovable. Furthermore, scholars sometimes complained that he is insufficiently diplomatic, as when he writes that any hundred historians give less than one percent of their space to motivation, that "expect[ing] the average historian to do psychohistory is like trying to teach a blind man to be an astronomer."[7] Most academic historians working closely with deMause feel insulted by such analogies, and I believe that the disdain for academics deMause often slips into is connected to the disappointment he experienced at Columbia.

Critics of Volkan, including those associated with Lifton's Center on Violence and Human Survival, have focused on his failure to publically take a moralistic approach to the perpetrators of some of the horrors of our modern world, especially the slaughter of Armenians in World War I. However, this runs counter to his goal of persuading both parties in conflicts to speak to him, and ultimately their own enemies, in the process of humanizing the other.

One crucial way of determining the influence of an intellectual leader is the number of books written, the influence of those books, and the continuity of the institutions created. In terms of publications, including co-authored and edited volumes, Volkan is the most prolific with fifty-eight books—many in foreign languages—followed by Lifton with twenty-eight and deMause with eight. In terms of the academic acceptance and influence of these volumes, Lifton has had the most influence, then Volkan, and finally deMause. On the Internet, deMause's approach to psychohistory remains strong. Regrettably, Lifton's Center on Violence and Human Survival ceased to exist as such after he left it in 2002, and Wellfleet has also met the same fate because there was no plan for a transition to younger leadership. The failure of the center Volkan established, and of the journal he created, to survive long after his retirement from the University of Virginia is a negative indication for the continuation of his work. Yet the acclaim he receives around the world, as indicated by his multiple nominations for the Nobel Peace Prize and the large number of colleagues willing to write tributes honoring him for a *Clio's Psyche* Volkan Festschrift,[8] is a positive indication for his continued influence.

There is a mixed record of continuity among the institutions deMause founded. The Psychohistory Press ceased publishing long ago and his Institute for Psychohistory meetings were discontinued three decades ago, but his journal continues and the IPA remains active. Indeed, there are positive indications that a younger generation of colleagues is assuming leadership roles in the association. All three have contributed to our understanding of group phenomena and are committed to lessening violence in our world. Lloyd deMause has proudly advocated psychohistory as an independent scientific discipline while Lifton and Volkan are committed to applied political psychology/psychohistory focused on problems of hatred and violence, with Volkan taking his intellectual ideas to the actual hot spots from which violence springs.

Notes

1 This led to the publication of *Thought Reform and the Psychology of Totalism: A Study of "Brainwashing" in China* (1961).
2 Although Lifton's group ceased to meet at Wellfleet as its founder approached his ninetieth year, it has met informally on an annual basis for lunch in New York City where he currently lives.
3 Lifton, *Witness to an Extreme Century* (2011): p. 48.
4 *Thought Reform and the Psychology of Totalism* (1961); *Death in Life: Survivors of Hiroshima* (1968); *The Nazi Doctors: Medical Killing and the Psychology of Genocide* (1986).
5 David Beisel, "Genocidal Agenda: Witnessing the Role of the Nazi Doctors," *Clio's Psyche*, Vol. 19 No. 2 (September 2012): p. 170.
6 *The History of Childhood* (1974); *A Bibliography of Psychohistory* (1975); *The New Psychohistory* (1975); *Jimmy Carter and American Fantasy: Psychohistorical Explorations* (with Henry Ebel, 1977); *Foundations of Psychohistory* (1982); *Reagan's America* (1984); *The Emotional Life of Nations* (2002); and *The Origins of War in Child Abuse* (2010).
7 Lloyd deMause, "Independence of Psychohistory," *Foundations of Psychohistory* (1975).
8 Volkan's September 2013 Festschrift had twenty-six articles by twenty-eight authors, with two more articles included in the subsequent issue.

8

OUTSTANDING PSYCHOHISTORIANS GAY, LOEWENBERG, AND BINION

Rudolph Binion (1927–2011), Peter Gay (1923–2015), and Peter Loewenberg (1933–) are the three most outstanding and well-known psychohistorical historians.[1] I am fortunate in having had the pleasure to know, respect, and learn from all three. There are many similarities among these historians of modern Europe. They are all excellent scholars steeped in modern European culture and history. The two Peters were born in Germany. Rudolph, though born in New York, traveled in Europe as a boy, lived in Europe as a young man, and was able to lecture in French, German, and Italian, as well as in English. Naturally, they had somewhat different areas of interest within their field. Gay focused mostly on the eighteenth century, the Enlightenment, bourgeois society of the nineteenth century, Freud, and the pleasure wars. His monumental five-volume study, *The Bourgeois Experience: Victoria to Freud* (1984–1998), includes *The Education of the Senses* (1984), *The Tender Passion* (1986), *The Cultivation of Hatred* (1993), *The Naked Heart* (1995), and *Pleasure Wars* (1998). It is an extraordinary scholarly accomplishment. Gay worked through many of his negative feelings toward Germans before he could write on Germany itself. Loewenberg has focused on Austrian socialists, China, highly creative groups, psychoanalysis, psychohistory, and the Nazis. Binion, also a modern historian, wrote quite extensively about varied themes, including the eroticization of death in the Middle Ages, Hitler and his relationship with Germans, group process, Pirandello, Lou Salomé, and leaders.

My relationship with these three talented contributors to psychological history impacts how I see them, what I know about each, and what I am able to write about them. As was the case of others in the IPA, I started out in awe of Rudolph Binion, with my admiration reflecting some fear of a brilliant man who had a named professorship (a rarity in the IPA) and who could be difficult at times. When Lloyd deMause, as his publisher, made the most minor of changes,

Professor Binion, on vacation in Sicily at the time, read the galleys and traveled a considerable distance to fax and telephone deMause to berate him, insisting on the restoration of the very minor changes in his text. On another occasion, he had a publisher withdraw a book as a result of a minor mistake made by a proofreader. As editor of *Clio's Psyche* I established the "Binion Rule," under which no dot was added and no "t" crossed without the expressed agreement of the author, and we applied it to very few authors. I discovered only much later how carefully Rudy (all of his friends called him Rudy) went over his writing. Binion was a loyal supporter of *Clio*, declaring that "my other journals pile up, but *Clio* I read from cover to cover." We became good friends and, as a friend and editor, I came to see his human frailties as well as his warmth, wit, and erudition.

Peter Loewenberg was at the Stockton 1976 psychohistory conference, as I was, but I only met him in 1982 when I, together with David Beisel and Henry Lawton, went to his Rutgers University psychohistory lecture, making a point of introducing myself to begin a professional relationship. He joined the Psychohistory Forum and has always been a strong supporter of this group. In 1989 he invited me to present at the International Society of Political Science meetings in Israel and I accepted. Despite the geographical distance between northern New Jersey where I live and Southern California where he makes his home, we have had a cordial professional relationship and I greatly admired his scholarship that appeared in the *American Historical Review*, *Decoding the Past*, and elsewhere.

Geographically, Peter Gay may have lived the closest to me of these three (a mere ninety miles away), but emotionally and intellectually he was the most distant. Indeed, when I had a National Endowment for the Humanities Summer Fellowship at Yale University in 1980, it never crossed my mind to try to visit him. Gay was already famous when I was a graduate student in his field of modern European history with favorable reviews of his books in the *New York Times*, but I felt little connection to him and what he wrote. I am not sure why this was the case. Perhaps there was an element of envy or that someone I respected at the time disparaged his work. The polite but consistent "no thank you" letters and notes I got in response to my invitations to him to speak at Ramapo College, the Psychohistory Forum, and the IPA certainly did not make me feel more connected to him. When I finally interviewed Gay in 1997 in the presence of one of his former graduate students, I found him to be informative but distant. Now, as I review his body of work, I am enormously impressed with the breadth and depth of his erudition and his contribution to psychological history. Below I will separately discuss the lives and work of all three modern European historians and add more comparisons.

Born as Peter Joachim Fröhlich in Berlin on June 20, 1923, the future Peter Gay was the only child of a manufacturer's representative for a number of companies who dealt with large department stores. His father was awarded the Iron Cross Second Class because he had shed blood for his country in the First World War. His mother was a housewife and a lovely looking woman who suffered from ill health her entire life, including bouts with tuberculosis. When he was about nine-and-a-half years old, the Nazis came to power, making a big difference in his life because his family, who saw themselves as German, were now seen as hated Jews. He said, "It was very isolating and difficult to deal with because I was constantly being called names" and was "complicated by the fact that I continued in a . . . Gymnasium [high school], and stayed there for five years during that period."[2] Compared to the beatings and hatred directed at other Jews, as a boy Gay said that he had a relatively easy time under the Nazis. This was made possible mostly because of his father's strategy of finding interesting alternate activities to discourage brooding about the difficult situation the family faced.

Father and son were impassioned soccer fans, so they focused on the Sunday games as one of their "survival strategies." They also became passionate stamp collectors. His father was very active in planning to get the family out of Nazi Germany, although that would not be until close to the start of World War II. Peter greatly admired his father's initiative and mentioned never rebelling against him, but rather identifying with him. For example, "He was a village atheist of the most extreme kind, and so am I and have always been."[3] The family members were patriotic Germans who became Jews by decree when Hitler came to power.[4] Hitler's rise to power shocked the family, but they were able to maintain the appearance of a fairly normal life until 1939, when the Nazis' decrees took away the family business and the senior Fröhlich was betrayed by the gentile partner he had taken as a way of getting around anti-Jewish decrees.

In Gymnasium, Peter did not suffer much overt anti-Semitism, although when he did, it was instigated by a particular member of the Hitler Youth. Without consciously doing so, he made himself second in the class to this young Nazi, even though he was brighter. Gay reports, "This act of self-protection had become second nature to me."[5] Unlike some of their close relatives, the family barely escaped before the war started, at first to Cuba and then in 1941 to Denver, where Peter graduated from the University of Denver. In *My German Question: Growing Up in Nazi Berlin* (1998), Fröhlich, whose family changed their name to Gay in the U.S., outlines his experiences. Fröhlich means happy, but Peter was carrying around too much repressed anger to be happy. His anger took the form of hatred toward Germans for what they had done to his family and him, including a desire to kill. For a long time "the only good German to him was a dead German."[6] His autobiography is about the almost six years of his life that he spent under Hitler, and it begins with the intense anger he felt for Germans in 1961 when he traveled to a conference in Berlin.[7] Ultimately, Peter Gay came to relinquish some of this anger. Perhaps this had to do with his five times a week analysis when he was in psychoanalytic training in his forties and fifties.

Peter Gay became a graduate student at Columbia University in 1946, started teaching there in 1947, and earned his political science doctorate in 1951. In 1952, his dissertation, *The Dilemma of Democratic Socialism: Eduard Bernstein's Challenge to Marx*, received excellent reviews when published, yet a few years later he was passed over for promotion. He said he once again felt like a refugee and ultimately found refuge in Columbia's History Department where close friends, especially Richard Hofstadter, were able to obtain for him a position in modern European history.[8] Fortunately, Gay was a quick study, learning the standards and methods of the historical profession.

About thirty books were written, edited, or co-authored by this man, who reported that "Freud said that the most effective—or rather, the least ineffective—way of dealing with misery is work, and I can testify that he was right."[9] But work was not primarily a way of getting away from misery, since Gay affirmed, "I have at times been accused of being a workaholic. I must plead guilty to the charge that it is undisturbed working time that makes me happy. The traditional division between work and play does not really fully apply to me."[10] As an organizer of history lectures at Ramapo College, I can vouch for the difficulty of getting Gay to leave his work, even as I offered large sums of money as speaker's honoraria to no avail. His writing was made easier because he reports that "I took to English as though it were my mother tongue" and "I fell in love with the [English] language and came to regard it as an incomparable vehicle for expression."[11] He also found love in his life when he married Ruth Slotkin Glazer, who was divorced from the famous sociologist Nathan Glazer and had three daughters under ten years old. Gay, in his words, was a lifelong "non-Jewish Jew" and as a youngster said he would only marry a gentile, but after the anti-Semitism he experienced in Nazi Germany, he married a Jew and wrote extensively about German-Jewish adaptations, including Jewish self-hatred.[12]

Peter Gay's opus is so voluminous and varied that there is not space to discuss his books in more than passing. His early books were mostly devoted to Voltaire, the French Enlightenment, and the French Revolution. Gay's early aversion to Germans meant that those he wrote about he saw as "good" Germans, including the democratic Marxist Jew Eduard Bernstein and the democratic Germans in *Weimar Culture: The Outsider as Insider* (1968). The 1968 student riots at Columbia University led to him leaving for Yale the following year, where he held the Durfee and then the Sterling professorships. The German refugee scholars Franz Neumann and Herbert Marcuse first introduced him to Freud. Following his six or seven years of training at the Western New England Institute for Psychoanalysis, he wrote eight books with Freud in the title, as he defended the creator of psychoanalysis in an era of Freud bashing.[13] Unlike his friend Loewenberg, Gay did not want to take time from his scholarship to see patients and complete his psychoanalytic training. Gay lamented that neither historians nor psychoanalysts read his *Freud for Historians* (1985), which my students had trouble reading and I also found disappointing. Among the activities of his extremely productive retirement was serving as the founding director of the New York Public Library's Center for Scholars and Writers (1997–2003). Although Peter Gay was using a walker six years before his death, Ken Fuchsman remembers him at a public meeting being articulate and insightful in his defense of Freud.[14]

Now I will turn to Peter Loewenberg, another German-born Jew who has contributed so much to psychohistory. As reported by his eldest son Samuel, "Peter Jacob Loewenberg was born into [the] turbulence" of the year Hitler came to power, and unlike most German Jews, his parents were determined to flee as soon as possible.[15] Six weeks after being born in August 1933 in Hamburg, he was on a ship to Shanghai. This was precipitated by Nazi legislation forcing his father out of the psychiatry department at the University of Hamburg. His "Mom," Sophie, was an idealistic, socialist, public health nurse who converted to Judaism from Lutheranism and his "Father,"[16] Richard, was the humanist son of a liberal Jewish writer, poet, and educator. He realized the urgency of the situation but was determined to find entry into a country where his psychiatric credentials would be accepted without professional retesting. Fortunately, the family was able to find this and join the Jewish colony in Shanghai, where he was soon learning Chinese as he worked both as a physician and psychiatrist in what he thought would be his permanent home. Turbulence followed the little family with the Japanese invasion of China, and the Loewenbergs were then on their way to California.

Safely away from German Nazis and Japanese fascists, the family had a tough struggle in the Great Depression as Sophie commuted a long distance to work as a night nurse and Richard worked 120 hours a week as an intern, being paid for a mere twenty-five hours a month, as he struggled to gain recertification. Little Peter had to spend a painful year with a pediatrician's family away from his parents due to their situation. By 1944, the Loewenbergs moved to Bakersfield and life became more normal. There, son Peter became a bar mitzvah and won the class prize in U.S. history, as well as a national *Time Magazine*-sponsored current affairs contest. His mother was active in Jewish affairs and in the cause of social justice. Farm worker organizer Cesar Chavez recuperated from a hunger strike at the Loewenbergs' home. Peter went to Bakersfield College and then the University of California at Santa Barbara, majoring in history and political science. He went to graduate school, studying diplomacy at the Berkeley campus of the University of California. Then his world fell apart when his father suddenly died of a stroke at fifty-six. Depth psychotherapy helped the young man with his depression and search for identity. Therapy also led him to switch to cultural and intellectual history, where there was room for more in-depth explanations than in diplomacy. After taking his doctoral degree, he went to study at the Free University of Berlin and then trained in psychoanalysis in Los Angeles after he had a teaching position.

Peter Loewenberg has had a dual career as a historian and psychoanalyst with a powerful commitment to psychohistory. He is a strong believer in the complete integration of these two disciplines. Loewenberg took his history doctoral degree in 1966 and taught European intellectual and cultural history; German, Austrian, and Swiss history; as well as political psychology and psychohistory in the History Department of UCLA from 1965 until his final retirement in 2004. Once he had his degree and full-time employment, Peter went into analytic training for eight years. Under California law, he was able to earn a doctoral degree in psychoanalysis in 1977. To this day, Loewenberg is a training and supervising analyst at the New Center for Psychoanalysis. To assist in the integration of these disciplines, Loewenberg has taken a leadership role with considerable success. For example, he was the primary author of the 1977 California Research Psychoanalyst Law, which allowed academics in anthropology, history, literature, and other disciplines to practice psychoanalysis to further their research. He also chaired the Research Clinical Training Committee to further the training of UCLA faculty members from numerous departments. In 1993, he co-founded the University of California Interdisciplinary Psychoanalytic Consortium comprised of numerous clinicians who meet annually at the UCLA Conference Center, located on the shores of Lake Arrowhead in the San Bernardino Mountains for a (sometimes university-funded) three-day research workshop. Loewenberg arranged for low cost therapy for graduate students and enabled some to augment their UCLA history coursework with seminars at the psychoanalytic institute.

A major contribution Loewenberg made was as Dean of the Southern California Psychoanalytic Institute from 2001–2006. He negotiated the re-unification of the two Los Angeles institutes that had split in 1950 into the New Center for Psychoanalysis in Los Angeles. This act of skillful diplomacy freed considerable funds when one of the buildings was sold to support psychoanalytic training. It is further evidence of his practical approach as an institution builder. As chair of the International Psychoanalytic Association China Committee, he has led an important development in opening the land he lived on for four of his earliest years to psychoanalysis and potentially psychohistory. To further psychoanalysis and psychohistory, Loewenberg travels to many different parts of the world.

As a psychohistorian in 1971, under the editorship of Peter Gay's friend Robert Webb, Loewenberg was able to publish the pathbreaking articles, "The Unsuccessful Adolescence of Heinrich Himmler" and "The Psychohistorical Origins of the Nazi Youth Cohort" in the prestigious *American Historical Review*. Besides numerous articles, he published the book *Decoding the Past: The Psychohistorical Approach* (1985, 1996), which I used successfully in my psychohistory course. He has written a large variety of articles, some of which were collected in *Fantasy and Reality in History* (1995). More recently, with Nellie Thompson, a former student, he edited *100 Years of the IPA: The Centenary History of the International Psychoanalytical Association 1910–2010* (2011) with fifty-six contributors from forty-one countries and societies. He has also lectured or taught in America, Europe, Africa, Israel, Latin America, China, and Hong Kong.

Peter Loewenberg has been an elegant voice for both psychoanalysis and psychohistory. He sees analysis as:

> 1) a therapy; 2) a humane 21st-century world view which bears both the tolerance of Enlightenment secularism and the Romantic assertion of human individuality; 3) an investigative research method; and 4) a mode of perceiving human interactions, data, events, and behaviors.[17]

The experience of therapy is a requirement for the understanding and the full use of categories 2–4. I understand this very well, because as a young professor searching psychoanalytical and psychohistorical sources, I kept looking up the meaning of transference to no avail. I had to experience the transference in my own training analysis to finally understand it. He calls for "a dual discipline and a dual career" with the clinician/researcher integrating knowledge of his dual training to see that which others miss. He seeks not an interface of knowledge, but rather an amalgam, a blending of the two. Both history and psychoanalysis are historical in their approach as they search beneath the surface to get to an understanding of the irrational. Loewenberg writes and speaks as a champion of psychohistory and proudly wrote that psychohistory has been offered as a field of doctoral study in history at Boston University, Kansas State, MIT, SUNY—Stony Brook, UCLA, and Yale.

Rudolph Binion is the third of these psychohistorians. He was born in New York City as the second son and youngest of three children to a mother who left the Jewish ghetto of Odessa in Ukraine at age five and a Hungarian nobleman who arrived in America in 1910 at the age of twenty-five. Both music and literature were important to the family. His mother worked for a literary magazine as a proofreader and secretary; his father, who was quite musical, became a circulation manager at Hearst publications and later started a business raising money to start Catholic colleges. Business and probably another family kept his father in Chicago most of the time—Binion told a friend that his parents were not married because his father already had a family. Although Binion had a fond memory of his father helping him with his homework, he died when the boy was thirteen, preventing a closer relationship. At an early age, Rudy had an adored German nanny, who cared enough about him to visit him in Paris decades later. His mother and her three children lived in the Pocono Mountains of New York State for the sake of the health of his older brother, and then after the death of his father they moved to Brooklyn. There were times when the Binions had lots of money, but they also experienced leaner times, especially after the death of the family breadwinner. Binion's mother did some export/import business, taking him to Europe with her; Europe was an important part of his consciousness from an early age. He loved to read and his sister reports that travel created his interest in history.

Binion attended public schools in New York State and graduated from James Madison High School with a most distinguished group of alumni (two current senators and four Nobel Prize winners) in Brooklyn in two years after scoring very high on the Regents examination. As a student at Columbia University, he was mentored by Jacques Barzun, who later became one of the most severe critics of psychohistory. Binion earned the following degrees: a BA in 1945 after attending Columbia College for three years, a Diplôme in 1949 from the Institut d'Études Politiques in Paris (1947–1949), and a doctoral degree from Columbia University in 1959, which he also attended in 1946–1947 and 1953–1958. His education was interrupted by service in the United States Army in 1945–1946 and work as a statistical assistant for UNESCO in Paris from 1950–1953. Binion taught at Rutgers (1955–1956), MIT (1956–1959), Columbia (1959–1967), and Brandeis (1967–2011) universities. At Brandeis he was the Leff Families Professor of Modern European History, and in 1980 he was a guest professor at the Collège de France.

Professor Binion was widely recognized as brilliant, erudite, enthusiastic, humorous, innovative, inquisitive, perfectionistic, sometimes difficult, and warm-hearted. There was a certain duality to his personality; indeed, in a poem he wrote, titled "My Own Identical Twin," he referred to himself as "my own identical twin" and concluded, "I know not which is me."[18] There is no question about his unusual capacity for friendship and mentorship. Binion was extraordinarily generous in not only mentoring his students, but also fellow scholars, including independent scholars such as Jay Gonen, Deborah Hayden, David Lewis-Hodgson, and George Victor, who shared some of his interests. Despite his ill health, he provided historical details on Hitler to the psychiatrist and novelist Irwin Yalom. His friendships stretched far and wide, reflecting his openness to different cultures and his willingness to travel around the world to give distinguished lectures as well as to pursue his own research. He was quite comfortable inviting colleagues to sleep on his couch in Brookline, MA and when giving talks, despite his bad back, offered to sleep on the couches of colleagues such as me. Rudy maintained contact with an enormous number of his former students and colleagues. So many of them were awed by his brilliance and the range of his knowledge and colleague-ship and were pleased to call him a friend. Although he taught at prestigious universities, he never fell into the trap of academic snobbery, in which friendship and attention are focused more on prestigious academic settings and less on those who did not ascend far up the academic ladder.

Rudolph Binion reported coming to psychohistory because a student asked him about Freud and he started reading the founder of psychoanalysis.[19] He was unusually straightforward about his intellectual transformation within psychohistory. Binion had "originally taken psychoanalysis as the orthodox straight approach to understanding human life" and so was "an out-and-out Freudian."[20] However, as someone who had no psychoanalytic training and no therapy, he thought he could psychoanalyze as a purely intellectual endeavor both a historical subject like Frau Lou and a young lady of his "close acquaintance."[21] Not realizing that psychoanalysis is not possible without an analyst ("the transference object" in psychoanalytic terms), he initially believed Lou Salomé's claim to have analyzed herself in print and felt deceived when he realized that she had recreated her history to fit a Freudian mode. Like Nietzsche, he felt betrayed by Frau Lou[22] and decided to put in the conclusion of Frau Lou "that my whole method was wrong."[23] He found himself "a revisionist Freudian psychobiographer," using this approach in his work on Hitler and Leopold II of Belgium, but he eventually came to believe that applied psychoanalysis was "a big mistake."[24] To Binion, "psychoanalysis was the childhood of psychohistory."[25] In his later years, he especially came to appreciate the work of Pierre Janet.

Focusing on traumatic reliving was a creative way to turn his psychohistorical talents to groups, avoiding the difficulties of uncovering the traumas of childhood and of unreliable recollections of it, such as Frau Lou's. Only a small number of colleagues had tackled group psychohistory, and none consistently brought the extraordinary depth of cultural, demographic, and historical knowledge to the task like Binion. Rather unusual for a professional historian, he believed in the independence of psychohistory, rather than seeing it as a subfield of history. Had he the health and time, he would have liked to apply his theory of traumatic reliving to some aspects of the recent history of the Middle East.

The ideal that Rudolph Binion lived by as a historian, psychohistorian, and scholar was to follow the evidence to its conclusion, no matter the cost. In writing about Hitler and other subjects, he held to this standard. In *Clio's Psyche*, which he served excellently as a member of the Editorial Board and as a trusted advisor, our goal is to provide as full a sense as possible of what a colleague was like as a person. What this means for Rudolph Binion is that I write honestly about all the aspects of his personality, not simply his strengths. He embraced this principle in *Clio's Psyche*.

As a human being, Binion was subject to the frailties that come easily to humans, which he explored so well in his books. Based on my long friendship with him, I felt that he could be envious without realizing it; it is my impression that it was due to his lack of analysis. As a teacher, he could start out by being so intimidating that Jacques Szaluta, a former graduate student of his at Columbia, reported that another seminar member left the course and university after being critiqued. Peter Loewenberg, who has had a most distinguished and productive career, was deeply offended when a letter of recommendation he requested from Professor Binion was positive, but written so as to weaken his candidacy for the particular position he sought. Rudy volunteered to review a colleague's book that he had praised privately, and then was highly critical of it. Our friendship blossomed despite his being markedly critical of some of my work on Jimmy Carter's childhood, and I found him to be an excellent friend. Sometimes, with his usual engaging manner and high-pitched voice, and in this case with a conspiratorial tone, he spoke of our "dark art" of psychohistory.

Binion's best work came when he trusted his intuition, utilizing family and adolescent materials as well as adult trauma, such as in the case of Adolf Hitler. *Hitler Among the Germans* (1976) is an extraordinary work that combines these elements with incredible archival research that took him to East Germany during the Cold War. As with his *Frau Lou: Nietzsche's Wayward Disciple* (1968) book, this tour de force also created many problems for Binion because some of what he wrote was misinterpreted—some thought he was blaming Dr. Bloch, the Jewish doctor who treated Hitler's mother, Klara, for breast cancer, for Hitler's irrational hatred of Jews and the Holocaust.

Binion's twelve books are a reflection of his in-depth scholarship. He also delighted in genuine intellectual exchange, which was his forte. This was reflected in his four symposia published in *Clio's Psyche* from 2000–2010, a period in which his health was declining.[26] These symposia were "Group Psychological Symposium" (December 2000); "De Gaulle as Pétain" (September 2005); "What Made Europeans European" (June 2009); and "Reliving with Freud" (June/September 2010).

The two Peters were analyzed and trained in psychoanalysis at length, although Gay chose not to take time from his research and writing to see patients. In contrast, Binion had no training or analysis, which is related to his having had such difficulty when he tried to be a rigid Freudian while writing about Lou Salomé. Turning to traumatic reliving allowed him to avoid some of the same pitfalls. Loewenberg came to psychoanalysis earliest during his treatment following symposia in *The Journal of Psychohistory* and elsewhere. His work in some articles, such as in his piece on King Leopold of Belgium and Bismarck's "Alliance Nightmare" (June 2005) is brilliant. At age eighty-four Rudolph succumbed to his many illnesses after having his wife send out an affectionate note to his friends, bidding them farewell.

All three European historians made major contributions to psychohistory, although Peter Gay thought of himself as doing "history informed by psychoanalysis," because he rejected what he called "the historical reductionism of psychohistorians, however interesting and even important it can be, [it] cannot by its nature unmask the past in all its dimensions."[27] Unlike his colleagues, Binion was never analyzed, distrusted analysis, and became quite uncomfortable with psychoanalysis as the basis of psychohistory and liked Lloyd deMause's idea of it being a separate discipline.

All three were born Jews. Binion, who had no use for religion, told me he was only Jewish according to Hebraic law; that is, his mother was Jewish. He harbored a strong animosity toward Israel, which he never delved into, perhaps because that seemed inappropriate while teaching at a university founded specifically so Jews would not be discriminated against as they were elsewhere at the time. Gay was a German of Jewish descent who declared that he became a Jew by Nazi decree, but in his autobiography there is evidence of Jewishness within the family prior to that event, as indicated by Peter's circumcision, use of Yiddish terms, and his father's quiet following of Jewish rituals in mourning his own father. All three became atheists. In terms of birth order, the two born in Germany were only children, while the American born was the youngest of three children and the second son. All three idealized their fathers. All three married; Gay once, Loewenberg twice, and Binion three times. Binion was the most impulsive of the three, emailing a friend in California from the south of France to say that he just met in a museum the woman he would marry. He in fact did and had a good marriage with Eléna.

Of the three, I would say that Loewenberg is the most diplomatic, in that he was able to achieve the reunification of two rival Los Angeles psychoanalytic institutes and to work in Chinese culture, which requires utmost diplomacy. Gay was certainly the next most diplomatic, as when he set up the New York Public Library's special program for scholars and writers. Diplomacy was not Rudy Binion's forte; indeed, he could be very undiplomatic. In my experience with him, Loewenberg has always been a good listener and a very friendly and supportive colleague. In my limited contact with Gay, he was very businesslike. Binion had a contagious exuberance.

All three have won far too numerous awards and honors throughout their careers to be mentioned here. To just name a few, Peter Gay won a National Book Award in History and Biography and an American Historical Association Award for Scholarly Distinction. Peter Loewenberg won a Sabshin Award for excellence in teaching psychoanalytic concepts and was named a Sir Peter Ustinov Visiting Professor at the University of Vienna in 2006. Rudolph Binion won a Charles Beer Prize of the American Historical Association and an American Council of Learned Societies Fellowship. In terms of worldwide reputations, Gay's is probably the most extensive, although Loewenberg's outreach to China may be reason to question this. In terms of historical productivity, Gay wrote the most books, followed by Binion. Loewenberg did much of his research in the consulting room as well as in archives. All had extensive professional friendships around the world. Psychohistory benefited enormously from all of their work, and I consider myself very fortunate to have known and learned from them, enabling me to pass on additional knowledge to my colleagues and students.

Notes

1 Peter Gay did not like the term psychohistorian, as I will discuss, but he certainly was one.
2 Paul Elovitz, David Felix and Bob Lentz, eds., "The Psychoanalytically-Informed Historian: Peter Gay," *Clio's Psyche*, Vol. 4 No. 2 (September 1997): p. 65.
3 Peter Gay, *My German Question: Growing Up in Nazi Berlin* (New Haven: Yale University Press, 1998): p. 48.
4 Gay, *My German Question*, p. 48.
5 Gay, *My German Question*, p. 62. I wonder if Gay identifying as a historian influenced by psychoanalysis rather than a more controversial psychohistorian was an adult version of this inclination to not stand out as a target.
6 Gay, *My German Question*, p. 202.
7 Gay, *My German Question*, pp. 1–7.
8 Peter Gay, "A Life of Learning," *American Council of Learned Societies Occasional Papers*, No. 58 (2004): pp. 1–2.
9 Gay, *My German Question*, p. 204.
10 Gay, "A Life of Learning," p. 18.
11 Gay, *My German Question*, pp. 116–117.
12 Gay, *Freud, Jews, and Other Germans: Masters and Victims in Modernist Culture* (New York: Oxford University Press, 1978).
13 Gay's *Freud: A Life for Our Time* (1988) is very well respected.
14 Ken Fuchsman, "Peter Gay (1923–2015): In Memoriam," *Clio's Psyche*, Vol. 22 No. 1–2 (June–September 2015): p. 118.

15 Samuel Loewenberg, "Loewenberg Early History," *Clio's Psyche*, Vol. 19 No. 1 (June 2012): p. 57.

16 Mom and Father are the terms Loewenberg used in an interview so I have left them as he wrote them.

17 Peter Loewenberg, "Professional and Personal Insights," *Clio's Psyche*, Vol. 4 No. 2 (September 1997): pp. 33–34.

18 Rudolph Binion, "My Own Identical Twin," *Clio's Psyche*, Vol. 18 No. 2 (September 2011): p. 209.

19 Bob Lentz, "The Courage of Rudolph Binion," *Clio's Psyche*, Vol. 1 No. 3 (December 1994): p. 8.

20 Rudolph Binion, "My Life with Frau Lou," in L.P. Curtis, Jr., ed., *The Historian's Workshop* (1970): p. 296.

21 Binion, "My Life with Frau Lou," pp. 304–05.

22 Deborah Hayden, "Rudolph Binion's Traumatic Encounter Frau Lou," *Clio's Psyche*, Vol. 18 No. 2 (September 2011): pp. 209–215.

23 Binion, "My Life with Frau Lou," pp. 293–306.

24 Lentz, "The Courage of Rudolph Binion," p. 8.

25 Lentz, "The Courage of Rudolph Binion," pp. 8–9.

26 Rudy had fought many a courageous battle for life and health. As a young man, he was stricken with life-threatening dysentery in Tunis and later in Mexico. In 1983 he survived a most serious bout with bowel cancer and sometime afterwards suffered from a botched operation on a broken hip and leg from a mugging. This was followed by extremely serious heart problems, while he also suffered from an excruciatingly painful back and gout. In his later years, he suffered from kidney stones, and because of kidney failure, he spent his final year on dialysis, administered at home by his wife Eléna—a nurse. In the end, his body could not tolerate the dialysis, several infections, pneumonia, and, finally, chronic heart failure.

27 Gay, "A Life of Learning," p. 11.

9

MY JOURNEY AS A PSYCHOHISTORICAL TEACHER

Helping students learn is a complex activity I have enjoyed and worked hard to achieve in the last fifty-five years. In searching my records, I have been surprised to discover that I have written fifteen chapters of books and articles about this process, as well as an equal number of professional presentations and workshops.[1] Teaching has not been easy, but it has usually been rewarding.

When I first began to teach, like most graduate students and newly minted doctorates, I followed the "teach them everything you learned in graduate school" model. I was going to stuff into the heads of the students as much as possible the materials that I had crammed into my own skull. In those early days, the students at Rutgers, Temple, and Fairleigh Dickinson universities and Middlesex Community College were usually not highly motivated because I was teaching required history courses on Western Civilization. Soon I began gradually, but drastically, to cut down on the amount of material I delivered and concentrate more on interesting historical individuals, as well as teachable moments. Such moments might occur because of something going on outside of class or a question. Students' fears of being drafted to fight in the growing war in Vietnam sometimes led to teachable moments regarding ordinary people in warfare. At the beginning of a lecture on Napoleon Bonaparte at Temple University, a student asked why the Emperor was portrayed as having his hand under his shirt on his stomach. We then had lots of fun coming up with different explanations. It was wonderful to see the students' faces light up and to see them want to go beyond the textbook to get more information.

I started teaching as a well-trained traditional historian focused on diplomatic, economic, military, and social history. However, as I read psychoanalysis and psychohistory at the Ambler Campus of Temple University and audited Sidney Halpern's classes, I gradually started teaching psychohistorically. This brings up the question, "What makes teaching psychohistorical?" While there is no one way to do and teach psychohistory, for me it involves a focus on some or all of the following: unconscious motivation, childhood, coping mechanisms, dreams, emotion, group fantasies and delusions, personality, and trauma. My turn away from traditional history was a gradual process, evolving over time, and influenced by the nature of the subject matter under consideration. Later I will discuss this more in terms of particular courses. I was amazed that my mentor, Halpern, told his Western Civilization II survey class (1400–present) that they would be focused solely on Marx, Darwin, and Freud, since I have always felt compelled to cover the listed time period and subject of the course I was assigned to teach. It wasn't simply that Halpern was so much more confident than me, but that my conscience dictated that I teach the course description—within which I had considerable leeway. By auditing this particular course, I learned the psychohistory of these three influential men and passed it on to my students after intensive reading of their works.

At Temple University I could only teach broad survey courses, which limited how much psychohistory I could bring into my classes. I was not inclined to make sweeping psychohistorical and other generalizations until later in my career. At Ramapo College, where in 1971 I became a founding faculty member, the scope for teaching psychohistory classes and teaching history psychohistorically increased immensely, although I continued to teach Western Civilization and eventually World History. My specifically psychohistorical courses are Children and Youth in History; Darwin, Marx, and Freud; Hitler, the Holocaust, and Genocide; the Psychology of Creativity; the Psychology of Political Leadership; Psychohistory; Psychohistory and Society; the Psychological Interpretation of Film; Identity; and the Psychology of Greatness.[2] Because of various changes at my college, temporarily I am now only teaching the Holocaust psychohistory class on a regular basis, yet every course I teach is permeated with psychohistory.

Much of my teaching has focused on issues of war and peace. It is my firmly held conviction that war should only be an option of last resort for civilized society. In modern Western society, and perhaps for all contemporary human beings, it is necessary to dehumanize and demonize before going to war. Fear encourages dehumanization, hatred, and the demonization of the potential enemy. To teach these concepts I used various techniques and materials, including films such as Sam Keen's *The Faces of the Enemy* (1987).

One of my goals as an educator is to help students recognize that they have a responsibility as human beings and as educated citizens to understand these processes, so as not to unthinkingly become a party to war or readily allow their country to be one. I do this in a variety of courses including: War, Peace, and Conflict Resolution; 9/11 and the Psychology of Terrorism; and Hitler, the Holocaust, and Genocide. An unusually perceptive student asked how in covering so much suffering, I avoid desensitizing my classes to violence in getting them to realize its complexities and magnitude. I tell my students that we are all participant-observers in the human condition and that includes the inclination to solve our problems through violence and war rather than understanding and negotiation. The Holocaust class ends with a debate on whether and in what time period humans can renounce genocide.

When George H.W. Bush prepared for war against Iraq in 1990, together with students I started the Emotions of War Research Project, which helped young people understand how emotions and emotional images are galvanized for promoting war.[3] As the second George Bush's administration ramped up for war in 2002, the students and I looked at the images in the news that evoked strong feelings of sympathy, support, condemnation, empathy, or disdain. I taught them that the choice of images displayed usually reflects the values and political preferences of the displayer. Even the apparently neutral ground that teachers and others would like to tread is laden with hidden emotional landmines. As a teacher, I confront these issues on a daily basis in a variety of courses.

In the classroom, I am often aware of a powerful student inclination to have only empathy or sympathy for one group of victims at a time. This may have something to do with why discussions of tragedies and injustices among groups and individuals may devolve into "victimization Olympics," an intense competition to prove that one's own group has suffered more than another group, which then justifies a greater sense of entitlement.

Students, like rivals in the Middle East, often treat victimhood as a zero-sum game in which concern for one group comes at the cost of the other. In teaching Hitler, the Holocaust, and Genocide for several decades, I had great difficulty getting students to empathize with the suffering of more than one group. It is important to mention that these students are representative of our student body, which means that they are overwhelmingly Christian in religion or background, with about ten percent being Jewish. There is an occasional Muslim who takes the class. Regardless of religion, for decades my classes normally resisted examining genocide other than that of Jews in the Holocaust. One of my great accomplishments was to use powerful images and especially readings on the victims of genocide in Rwanda, Cambodia, China, Bosnia, Armenia, and elsewhere to help students empathize with these victims, as well as with the Jewish victims of Nazi genocide.

When the "victimization Olympics" commence, I try to help students understand the extent to which groups who feel victimized may also feel entitled to special treatment and revenge. This sense of specialness is part of what motivates different groups to act inhumanely. I use examples from twentieth-century German and Balkan history, starting with Germans who felt victimized by the loss of World War I and the Treaty of Versailles. They then felt entitled to become a conqueror nation, lording it over other peoples whom they dehumanized, first through their propaganda and subsequently in reality. Another illustration is the Serbs, who felt justified in dominating, as well as ethnically cleansing, Croats and Muslims because of their own suffering and frustrated nationalism under the Ottoman Turks, Austrians, and Nazis during World War II.[4] Understanding these historical examples and the emotions behind them helps students to understand their own feelings and to approach the course with a greater sense of empathy.

Mary Coleman and other colleagues at the International Psychohistory Association gave me tremendous insight into killing and war, and I quickly brought it into my classes. We live in a society that spews out so many fantasies about killing and war on television, in the movies, and in fiction that students are not aware of the reality. They have the fantasy that humans, especially men, kill with ease for the flimsiest of reasons. The reality is that killing is something that most healthy people do not readily do, not even in wartime. In World War II, the U.S. military historian Colonel (later General) S.L.A. Marshall found that in the European theater of conflict, only fifteen to twenty percent of American soldiers actually discharged their weapons in combat, although most had the opportunity to shoot. He did not call the other eighty to eighty-five percent cowards, just good Americans who were more willing to risk being killed than to violate the "thou shalt not kill" teachings of their parents, teachers, coaches, youth leaders, ministers, priests, and rabbis.

Students have difficulties accepting the reality of these inhibitions. In the second class of the course War, Peace, and Conflict Resolution, I tell the students that war is about killing, and then ask the question: "Under what circumstances would you kill another human being?" Subsequently, I inquire as to how they think it feels to kill and then what students think the effects of killing would be on themselves and their society, both immediately and in the future. The idea is to get students to be less unrealistic about killing, violence, and war. My hope is that they will then become much more cautious about war. They then eagerly read *On Killing* (1995) by a soldier-psychologist, Dave Grossman, which helps them to understand the psychological effects of killing and warfare, with special reference to the war in Vietnam. They are taught about the human defense mechanisms of denial, intellectualization, repression, and so forth, which ultimately may result in traumatic reliving.[5] This is more than is subsumed under the title of Post-Traumatic Stress Disorder (PTSD). Because politicians and prominent soldiers often preface their warlike speeches with the statement that "nobody wants war," many students react with puzzlement when I refer to war as something that men enjoy and find meaningful.[6] I have some of them read Chris Hedges' *War as a Force That Gives Us Meaning* (2002) to understand this from the perspective of a *New York Times* foreign and war correspondent.

Whenever I can, I try to teach courses that seem relevant to the students, including courses on the presidential election every four years. I have often taught Leaders, Passion, and Success courses as a senior seminar, starting with the students writing a lengthy autobiography. The course was based on the Socratic dictum: "know thyself." This class was organized around them examining their lives and goals after graduation. I paid close attention to their individual aspirations and needs, personalizing their education, as I do whenever possible. Their final research paper was on a mentor or role model who has achieved what they aim to accomplish. The students saw it mostly as career development, while I saw it as applied psychohistory as they probed their own lives, personalities, skills, and dreams of success. They were motivated to do much more work than in a typical college course.

Another valuable senior seminar was September 11th and the Psychology of Terrorism, which I taught four times shortly after the terrorist attacks that shook the nation. It represented my commitment to utilize my knowledge of the past, as well as of human psychology, to shine a light on contemporary problems. To teach it, I drew on my experiences as a historian, a political science graduate student, a researcher on issues of war and peace, and a psychohistorian to help the students learn more about a terrifying, horrible subject. The students, some of whom could view the World Trade Center from their homes, probed issues of the life and motivation of Osama bin Laden and other terrorists, Islamic attitudes toward the West and modernity, President Bush as a war leader, and the prospects of the so-called "War on Terrorism." The problems and consequences of failed governments, international coalition building, the psychology of the suicide bomber, the human dimensions of tragedy, national mourning, and how the media treats a catastrophe like 9/11 were also foci of the course. In dealing with such painful contemporary materials, I sought to help students emotionally come to terms with the loss of security in our society and to heal. In 2003 I stopped teaching the course when student autobiographical accounts of the terrible events of 9/11 began to sound more like the national narrative and less personal.

Students can be quite resistant to learning because it involves hard work and giving up established ideas. Psychohistory provides enormous insight, but it can present an added dimension to this resistance because it often hits home on a personal level. For example, an earnest psychology student felt quite exposed as she read about and discussed with the class certain psychoanalytic concepts. She ultimately switched her major to literature, where she could study people at more of a psychological distance. To strengthen the history program, which did not have many majors, I started a history club and advised it for twenty years. Having numerous other psychohistorical pioneers, like David Beisel, speak at the college lessened student resistances since they could see that I was part of a significant movement in my psychological approach to knowledge.

Although I started my career giving lectures, I was never very comfortable with that traditional approach, because some students were too passive, which did not optimize learning. Soon I had my students sitting in circles or around conference tables to facilitate discussion. Eventually, I came to divide the students into small groups to discuss specific issues and then report back to the class as a whole. In my early days, I was amazed that girls almost always selected guys to lead the groups. When I pointed this out, more females took leadership roles. Historical re-enactment was a methodology I used extensively in the 1980s and 1990s. It was a lot of work, but it succeeded in motivating a greater interest in the subject as we assumed historical roles and enacted them in class. In recent years I have organized debates in most classes, which is an intense motivator for most students. They compete to give their best.

My journey as a professor helping young people learn has led me to teach numerous courses, which I have struggled and worked hard to make relevant to the lives of the students. For those who allow it, education can be transformative. In all of my classes, I have quickly learned the names of students and sought to deal with them as individuals. A basic principle of my pedagogy has always been to focus on the individual students and the emotions in the classroom. Psychohistory has improved my teaching and deepened my relationships with my students. In the process of teaching, I have learned an enormous amount and had some wonderful relationships with students, from undergraduate to postgraduate levels.

Notes

1 "Reflections on Psychoanalytic Education," *Viewpoints of Psychoanalysis* (May 1978): pp. 7–8; "Helping People Learn," *Psychohistory*, Vol. 3 No. 1 (1979): pp. 6–13; "Psychohistorical Teaching," *The Journal of Psychohistory* (Spring 1988): pp. 435–445; "Psychohistory in the Classroom," *The Journal of Psychohistory*, Vol. 15 No. 4 (Spring 1988): 340–347; "The Holocaust in the Classroom" and "Leadership Education," in Paul H. Elovitz, ed., *Historical and Psychological Inquiry* (1990): pp. 496–524; "War, Peace and Conflict Resolution—Researchers' Activities," *Clio's Psyche*, Vol. 1 No. 4 (March 1995): pp. 15–16; "A Unique Dual Education: Editor's Introduction and Personal Commentary," *Clio's Psyche*, Vol. 4 No. 2 (September 1997): pp. 36–41; "War, Trauma, Genocide, and Kosovo," *The Journal of Psychohistory*, Vol. 27 (Fall 1999): pp. 188–199; "Perspectives on Teaching About War-Making in 2002 America," *Clio's Psyche*, Vol. 9 No. 3 (December 2002): pp. 125, 140–144; "Teaching About War in Bush's 21st Century America," *The Journal of Psychohistory*, Vol. 31 No. 1 (Summer 2003): pp. 2–10, 35–48 (This invited article was the basis for a symposium issue with comments [pp. 11–48] by professors from nine universities and colleges); "A Dialogue on Online Education," *Clio's Psyche*, Vol. 12 No. 3 (December 2005): pp. 130–134 (with Kenneth Fuchsman [University of Connecticut]); "Psychohistorical Pedagogy," *Clio's Psyche*, Vol. 12 No. 4 (March 2006): pp. 205–207; "My Digital Generation of Students," *Clio's Psyche*, Vol. 21 No. 4 (March 2015): pp. 423–429; "Teaching the 2016 Election," *Clio's Psyche*, Vol. 24 No. 1 (Summer 2017): pp. 56–62. I also edited four student editions of *The Special Student Edition, 1994–1998* of *Clio's Psyche*, which were assigned in psychohistory courses.

2 One vital avenue for psychohistorical teaching was the senior interdisciplinary seminars, which were truly interdisciplinary until they were turned over to the majors in the twenty-first century. Under this aegis I taught courses such as the Psychology of Manhood, Presidential Elections, Psychohistory and Society, Leadership, and three more that I highlight in this chapter.

3 The students and I developed a survey of the emotions people felt and were able to get about a thousand responses from students and others throughout the United States, Europe, New Zealand, and Australia.

4 Vamık Volkan in his many books does an excellent job of describing this process and discussing the ways to avoid it.

5 Rudolph Binion's traumatic reliving scholarship is so much more complex and in depth than what is implied by the PTSD diagnosis, which grew out of the survivor's guilt work of William Niederland and others. Psychiatrists Chaim Shatan and Robert

Jay Lifton played a key role in getting PTSD put into DSM-III for the benefit of Vietnam veterans and others.

6 Mary Coleman, a longtime student of war and an anti-war demonstrator outside the White House, likes to point to the role of women in encouraging and enabling their men to go to war. Of course, now some women also fight as soldiers.

10

MY ROLE IN CREATING AND NURTURING POSTGRADUATE PSYCHOHISTORICAL EDUCATION

Scholars write books and articles. If they have appointments at major universities, they may mentor graduate students as part of their responsibilities. Some nurture the work of their friends. However, it is most unusual for one to organize meetings specifically designed to further the work of colleagues for over four decades and to edit a scholarly journal continually for a quarter century, all without remuneration. Since I am this scholar-organizer-editor, I ask myself: How did this come about and why? After describing what I do in creating and nurturing psychohistory, I will endeavor to explain my conscious and unconscious reasons for doing this.

Psychohistory offers unique insights into the human condition, yet it is seldom taught in graduate school.[1] Furthermore, in my experience, most scholars and clinicians become interested in psychohistory after they have earned their terminal degrees, rather than before. Mostly through my role as founder and convener of the Psychohistory Forum, I have sought to help fill the gap created by this situation by providing postgraduate education in this field.

Some of the subject matter presented at our intellectual forums is psychobiography—including presidential psychobiography and much, much more.[2] The subject is usually determined not by the organization, but by the scholar who is working to grow his or her knowledge.

My goal here is to first describe the mission of the Psychohistory Forum, which supports *Clio's Psyche*—its publication. The Forum's mission is to enlarge and disseminate the related paradigms of applied psychoanalysis, political psychology, psychobiography, and psychological history. We seek to do this by using non-technical language. Our charge is always to stimulate psychohistorical thought, publications, research, and teaching. As editor of *Clio* my specific objectives include communication with Forum members and networking with like-minded colleagues regardless of their geographical distance. I also help clinicians focus on history and current events, assisting academics in all disciplines—history, literature, political science, psychology, sociology, anthropology, and so forth—to utilize the insights and tools of psychoanalysis and psychology. Additional objectives of the Forum consist of fostering psychohistorical debate and discussion, transmitting the knowledge of an older generation of psychohistorians to those just entering the field, and researching and publishing the history of our field, thus memorializing the work of those who have built it. After describing its membership, I will describe the organization and methodology of the Saturday Work-In-Progress Workshops, the core of our postgraduate education.

The Psychohistory Forum is comprised of colleagues from a large number of fields. For example, at a particular Saturday seminar, two colleagues and I gave presentations on the 1970s as the age of guilt-evasion, narcissistic-permissiveness, and Watergate. Among the twenty-one colleagues exchanging ideas (allowing for multiple professional identifications) were thirteen therapists (eight psychoanalysts), seven professors, six psychologists, five historians, three social workers, two sociologists, and two MDs. The interdisciplinary cross-fertilization generated many ideas, encouraging additional research projects. Over half of the members of the Forum live too far away in North America to attend meetings. Not all of those in the Metropolitan New York area are able to attend meetings for a variety of reasons, such as having to see patients on Saturdays. Note that in following the model of the Institute for Psychohistory, I took the title of director, although in recent years I am as likely to refer to myself as the convener. While donating an enormous amount of time and energy to the group and its publication, like all other members I pay annual dues.

The Forum primarily meets on Saturdays in New York City four to six times a year. Because not everyone is free on Saturdays, and about a third of our members reside at a distance from Manhattan, we try to meet occasionally during the week and at other locations. Every year additional weekday meetings are held at international conferences. Typically, there is one at New York University during the International Psychohistorical Association (IPA) meetings. Others are held elsewhere at meetings of the International Society for Political Psychology and the Association for the Psychoanalysis of Culture and Society. Our presenters usually have terminal degrees (or certifications in the cases of practicing psychoanalysts) in their fields. One exception is a talented anthropologist named Eli Sagan who presented on the French Revolution and subsequently on Islamic fundamentalism. With only a bachelor's degree—albeit from Harvard—he taught at Brandeis, New School University, UC Berkeley, and elsewhere because of his brilliant scholarship. Some members join together on issues such as teaching or psychobiography and work in separate research groups. Because the main focus of our group is the development and exchange of ideas, impressive degrees and affiliations are never central to the work we do.

Our typical session focuses on only one presenter. Its outstanding aspect is that the colleague determines the subject matter. The director/convener, moderator, and the other participants of the Psychohistory Forum are there to help the presenter deepen his/her understanding of the subject. This is more akin to midwifery than to a senior faculty member helping a more junior colleague jump over the hurdles to complete a doctoral dissertation. The metaphor of midwifery is appropriate because as "midwives" and associates, we do not come up with the scholarly conception (the idea) for the research project presented, we do not do the research, we do not write the paper, and we do not do the difficult work of editing and revising. It is not our responsibility to do any of these things, though there are instances when we may help with them. Rather it is the conception of the presenter, which we are helping to birth into a healthy baby, in the hope it can grow to full adult form very quickly. In the process of doing this, we deepen our knowledge of the subject and usually have an interesting intellectual exchange.

Throughout this process, the presenter is in control. Because of this sense of control, s/he is willing to probe the subject more deeply. (Of course, the main issue is the presenter's personal motivation for examining the subject that makes it important enough to devote considerable time and energy to it.) That this in-depth examination can only occur in a safe environment goes without saying. This "safety factor" is absolutely essential: without it, the pangs of birth are so intense that an intellectual miscarriage may occur. A project for a book or scholarly article needs support; it can wither and die in the face of unwarranted criticism. The tenets of psychohistorical work include probing the materials in depth, following the emotion, and probing the author's transference to the subject matter and the group's countertransference feelings (the feelings induced in us by the materials and/or the presentation). Therefore, the presenter can feel and be quite vulnerable during the process, thus making safety all the more important.

Presenting at a Work-In-Progress Seminar can be invaluable to a scholar. The fact that the idea seems worthy of presentation gives validity to it and moves the researcher to work and write on it, or develop and polish it, if it has been languishing. There is confirmation in developing and presenting it. To a psychohistorical group, the presenter will normally start thinking and developing the idea along more psychological, or historical, principles. We encourage work on a specific, rather than a general, subject. A supportive group can validate many of the presenter's formulations. It can also offer possible solutions to problems encountered by the researcher. Ideas and relationships the researcher had not previously thought of come to the fore. Group members may identify emotions induced by the materials or stemming from the presenter's feelings toward the subject.

Interdisciplinary researchers and clinicians view the same subject content from many different and valuable angles. Even their off-the-mark suggestions can have value. In explaining why seemingly helpful suggestions do not work, the presenter is normally able to formulate a better understanding of his or her own brain child. Innovative ideas do not spring full-grown as from the head of Zeus, but are rather developed in stages. Any signs of criticism of the presenter, as opposed to analysis of the materials, are nipped early on by the director/convener, moderator, or group itself. In this process of nurturing a project, it is rewarding to watch it grow from a thought to an article and often ultimately to a book. This process of development is crucial to many presenters. Of course, there are presenters who want no more than a supportive group and are fairly limited in their goals.

To better describe how these Work-In-Progress papers work, I will identify some of the principles that govern the organization and guide the Forum.

- Our goal is never to state "the truth"; rather, it is to assist in probing how to strive to find "truths" useful for the presenter.
- The subject matter is determined by the presenter.
- Presenters approach their subject matter in different, quite individualistic, ways, and these variations are to always be respected.
- Case studies are preferred over more generalized studies.
- The presenter decides how much to bring to and take from the in-depth discussion.
- The presenter is in control at all times and may stop the process if so desired.
- Insight into the structure of the presentation is encouraged and criticism is discouraged.
- The group notes or analyzes the emotion in the room.
- If there are signs of the group becoming disputatious or critical, a member, or the convener, makes an interpretation, reminding the group of its standards.
- People work in quite different ways, and such variations are respected.
- Rigidity must be avoided.
- Ideas are to be nurtured, not stifled.
- Non-psychological explanations are not the main focus of our discussions.
- A major goal is to enlarge the psychological paradigm.

These principles enable our group to nurture psychohistorical knowledge. They were developed because of the pitfalls into which the Saturday Workshops of the Institute for Psychohistory fell. One problem was that presenters were occasionally attacked. Two occasions come to mind. A female medieval historian from western Pennsylvania came with a colleague to present her materials and members of the group attacked her, partly because her approach did not fit with that of Lloyd deMause. Consequently, no real psychohistory was done, and this colleague never returned. The second occasion involved a presentation by Reuben Fine, who was said to be deMause's psychoanalyst. The group was hostile to the presenter, which struck me as a displacement of anger toward deMause. I was frustrated and angered by failures of the group to live up to its potential. Therefore, when I started the Psychohistory Forum in 1982 with Henry Lawton as associate director, I determined that we would not make the same mistakes. With only one or two exceptions, we have lived up to our ideals.[3] I also decided that it would be mandatory for the presenter to have a paper that we vetted before sending it out to all Forum members prior to the meeting.

The relationship of *Clio's Psyche* to the Psychohistory Forum's Work-In-Progress seminars is complex. Our publication was created in 1994, initially to leave a record of our proceedings and to build the psychohistorical paradigm. Most publications growing out of Forum seminars appear in books or in lengthy articles much longer than those fitting into *Clio's* format and often being published in *The Journal of Psychohistory*. Indeed, as editor, I regularly publish my longer articles elsewhere. Within *Clio's Psyche*, the very numerous special features, special issues, and symposia of our scholarly quarterly have served to focus attention on enlarging the psychohistorical paradigm on issues such as apocalypticism, conspiracy theories, crime, cross disciplinary training, cyberspace, dreamwork, group process, home, humor, immigration, impeachment, imperialism, law, publishing, psychogeography, religion, serfdom, and societal change. Scholar/therapists have explored these subjects from extremely different viewpoints. The differences of opinion and even debates within our pages have helped enormously in building a sense of community.

Technology is offering us new opportunities to achieve our goals. Increasingly, our members meet electronically and our meetings are sometimes recorded and put on our website to be viewed by members-at-a-distance and others. Our website, cliospsyche.org, enables us to provide information to each other more efficiently and to introduce our work and aims to a much larger group of academics, clinicians, scholars, and students who otherwise might not know about it. Except for the issues published in the last year, all of our back issues are available at our website, cliospsyche.org. A goal of the website is to provide information on teaching psychological history as components of courses and in separate political psychology and psychohistory courses. Though the long-term consequences of this technological transformation remain to be seen, there is no question that it empowers more colleagues to participate and hone our craft.

Now, as promised at the beginning of this chapter, here is an exploration of my personal motivation as a nurturer of psychosocial knowledge, which fits in with the evolution of the Forum. When I started organizing the Forum over four decades ago, I was hesitant about becoming an author of books.[4] Writing was a chore for me and I suffered from writer's block. I was eager to learn from each of the numerous presenters, and my writing was limited to the presentation paper cover page with an invitation to attend the meeting, which was sent to each member of our group. Without immediately realizing it, I was following the model that I was learning in my psychoanalytic training—that is, of listening carefully and reflecting back to the author and group what I heard and then, when appropriate, to encourage them to look for deeper meanings in their materials. With some presenters who were initially shy about speaking, I encouraged them verbally and sometimes by writing an outline of their thoughts and ways in which I thought they might develop their ideas. Mostly, colleagues just needed to know that it was a safe environment in which to present. Colleagues came forth and at one point

I had a brochure with pictures of the presenters listing the meetings for the next two years.

Every four years we have presentations on the presidential candidates. This was a fascinating and time-consuming challenge. It also generated a fair number of articles by others and me because colleagues wanted to know what I had to say about the contenders and our future president. I came to realize that I benefit greatly from the stimulation of working with others; I was often slow to formulate my own ideas independently of the ideas of others. This was partly because I lacked confidence in my intelligence and originality. However, based on my training in history and psychoanalysis, I did have definite ideas about standards of evidence and the need of the psychological scholars to be aware of their own inclinations to project—what I like to call their own projective screens. To me it was fascinating to understand colleagues, especially what made them interested in a particular subject and what they were inclined to project onto the subject. In doing this, I was not judgmental. Increasingly, I came to realize our work, no matter what our field, tends to reflect our own inner needs.

So where did my own inner need to bring people together and nurture their work originate? Partly, it stemmed from as a child always seeing myself as an outsider and assuming the role of helper, especially to my mother who, as an early adolescent immigrant, aspired to knowledge despite having almost no formal opportunities to achieve it. I am living my mother's dream of education as a college professor and organizing and publishing psychohistory. As a midwife of knowledge I am continuing my childhood pattern of helping others. Thus I did not give birth to it, but I helped with its delivery. This is a feminine role, which is not usually valued in academia and educated circles generally, except perhaps at retirement parties. In delving into my reasons for assuming unusual and lengthy unpaid roles, I do not mean to discount the obvious regard I have received from many colleagues as leader of the Forum and as *Clio*'s editor. The respect of my colleagues is something I greatly value and which has made the hard work involved all the more gratifying.

It might seem likely that I would be bored after over four decades of doing this work. However, this is a rare occurrence because I am focused on aiding the struggle for greater insight rather than only on content, much of which I have heard before. If members of the group are bored by the presentations selected by the program committee and me, they express their concerns to me or simply do not return. Because the number of attendees is fairly stable, this does not appear to happen very often. Rather than being bored, I am tired of driving to Manhattan for Saturday meetings and have thoughts of having the meetings in my home where we have a lovely space that is larger than the one we usually pay to rent. Unfortunately, the members who live in Manhattan are not inclined to come to New Jersey and some lack automobiles.

As advocates of postgraduate interdisciplinary education, my colleagues and I at the Psychohistory Forum are interested in assisting in the building of the psychohistorical paradigm. Psychoanalysis, in its many varieties, is a vital tool, but it is only one among many. The psychohistorical work is what brings us and holds us together. *Clio's Psyche* is a consequence of this work, as is this book. My personal needs and passion to bring colleagues together to grow psychohistory has been crucial to this endeavor. Probing the childhoods, coping mechanisms, lives, traumas, and values of presidential candidates and presidents with my fellow citizens and psychohistorians has been a valuable way of continuing our postgraduate education.

Notes

1 This chapter is based on my article, "Postgraduate Psychohistorical Education," *Clio's Psyche*, Vol. 12 No. 3 (December 2005): pp. 113, 121–123.
2 Some other subjects include death, dying, and mourning; childhood and its history; war and peace; the history of psychohistory; the fathers and mothers of psychohistorians; right wing violence; 9/11 and the psychohistory of terrorism; millennialism; dreams; the role of countertransference; the uses and misuses of empathy; genocide and the Holocaust; post-traumatic stress disorder; men's envy of and attempt to subjugate women; film; sports psychology; guilt evasion and narcissism in the 1970s; and group process.
3 We failed abysmally when we ran a meeting on the psychology of sports. There were four presenters, only one of whom was a regular member of our group. Hardly any of our regular membership attended the meeting. One presenter savagely attacked another whose speech patterns he found to be frustrating. The attacker, who was behaving in a manner one would not expect from a psychoanalyst, was grieving the recent murder of his son, who had been involved in sports. In contrast, at the IPA I organized a meeting on sports psychology that was orderly and insightful.
4 I started to write a book on President Carter, but quickly dropped the project, as explained in the subsequent chapter.

11

THE DILEMMAS OF A PRESIDENTIAL PSYCHOHISTORIAN

As an American I have always been fascinated by our presidents, but as an English and European historian I never imagined myself writing on the American presidency. Nevertheless, I got started in this direction, which has resulted in numerous dilemmas and forty-three publications. At the summer 1976 Institute for Psychohistory meeting, there was enormous interest in the wake of Nixon's resignation and pardon as well as in the election itself. I was reading Jimmy Carter's campaign autobiography *Why Not the Best?* (1975) with great attention. At the meeting I said that this candidate is unusually revealing and that a psychohistorian should go down to Georgia and find out about his childhood and personality from those closest to him. Lloyd deMause, who had organized and chaired this meeting, declared, "Paul, you should go down to Plains." "Oh no!" I proclaimed, "I have my teaching, my patients, other responsibilities, and I can't afford the cost."

However, the seed was planted, and subsequently I was reading as much about Carter as possible. At the Stockton State national psychohistory conference later in the summer, I volunteered to talk about the Democratic nominee. As I walked with colleagues, the renowned psychohistorian/psychiatrist Robert Jay Lifton walked up behind me and put his hand on my shoulder saying, "You can't present on Carter!" I was virtually dumbfounded and don't remember what my response was beyond mumbling, "I committed to do it." He wanted me to abide by the Goldwater Rule—the unofficial name of the American Psychiatric Association's Section 7.3 ethics rule that forbids "commenting on individuals' mental state without examining them personally and being authorized by the person to make such comments." This rule was passed as a result of 1,189 psychiatrists, during the 1964 electoral campaign, declaring that Goldwater was psychologically unfit to be president in a survey published by *Fact Magazine*. The psychiatric community was embarrassed by this slandering of a presidential candidate and sought to prohibit it in the future. But I am not a psychiatrist, rather a historian, a serious scholar, and a citizen who was and is concerned that voters have full knowledge of whom they are electing. Consequently, I gave my well-received presentation on Carter that evening and began my career as a presidential psychohistorian. Lifton's failed attempt to dissuade me heightened my concern for ethical issues in our important work.

Robert Jay Lifton's concern for the good of the country led him to comment forty-one years later on Trump's mental state without a personal examination and a signed authorization from him. For example, in an Opinion Page letter to the *New York Times* editor titled "'Protect Us from This Dangerous President,' 2 Psychiatrists Say" (March 8, 2017), he questioned "Donald Trump's fitness for office, based on the alarming symptoms of mental instability." While he and his Harvard co-author asserted, "We are in no way offering a psychiatric diagnosis," they clearly were violating the spirit and letter of the Goldwater Rule. I applaud this action and similar actions of other psychiatrists who fear for our country.[1]

Lifton has more recently contributed to *The Dangerous Case of Donald Trump: 27 Psychiatrists and Mental Health Experts Assess Trump* (Thomas Dunne Books, 2017), edited by psychiatrist Bandy Lee, who organized Yale's "Duty to Warn" April 2017 conference. As much as I worry about our current president, I continue to remain troubled by the tendency to pathologize politicians because it can be misused for political purposes and it associates psychohistory with mental illness rather than creativity, innovation, overcoming trauma, and self-actualization.

Back in the summer of 1976 I remained hesitant about following through on my proposal to go to Plains to gather materials on Carter. Then I discovered my Institute for Psychohistory colleague David Beisel, also a European historian, had written a very fine article, "Toward a Psychohistory of Jimmy Carter," which prompted me to stop obsessing about the project and get to work on it. The results were a trip to Georgia and the article, "Three Days in Plains" (later a chapter of a book), and a fascinating encounter with people close to the future president. Despite feeling anxious, I considered the trip to be successful partly because I was able to use resistance analysis, which I was being taught in psychoanalytic training. Thus, when the future president's sister, Gloria Carter Spann, said that she was much too busy preparing for a party and an auction the next week to give me any time, I agreed that she was so busy that finding time would be difficult. Feeling somewhat understood, she then said, "Well, I'm going to the supermarket. I can pick you up and talk along the way. Where are you?" My response was that I was using the telephone outside of her brother Billy's gas station. When she arrived, she looked at me through her sunglasses, indicated for me to get in the car, and soon said, "How can a New York Jew understand anything about small-town Southerners?" My response was, "With your help I may be able to have some understanding." She then mentioned that recently Norman Mailer, who actually was a New York Jew as opposed to me, a Connecticut and New Jersey Jew, had been in Plains with his girlfriend and provided some interesting insights. We shared a common dislike for Mailer's tone and disagreed sharply about the cost of groceries as we chatted during her shopping, since as a farmer's wife she thought the prices were too low and I as a consumer thought they were too high. Yet she liked my directness.

While Gloria did not give me a lot of information on that occasion, unlike during the several hours spent interviewing her in her home the following year, she did strengthen my relationship with her mother. When I spoke to Lillian Carter, who was greeting tourists at the campaign trailer, she spoke highly of Gloria, whom she declared to be the smartest of her children. (I soon discovered that Lillian declared each of her offspring to be the smartest when she thought they needed more attention.) The strong, diminutive woman made an impact on me. "Don't shake my hand. See this big blotch on my hand? Someone must've stuck me with a pin and made this big bloodspot on my hand." She was very much in control. I felt for her because as I was about to enter the campaign trailer, a Southern man greeted me with a jolly slap on my back that left an imprint on the skin under my shirt. To me this was a reminder of the aggression released during presidential campaigns and why Lillian had to protect herself. Perhaps it also represented Southern feelings toward Northerners, even while they wanted our votes for one of their own.

In her home, "Miss Lillian" was both hospitable and quite manic. She offered to make dinner for me, which I declined and declined once more as I was trying to figure out how often you had to say no before Southerners stopped offering out of courtesy to a guest. I knew so little about Southern mores. Since I did not want to offend my hostess, I soon said yes (and in fact I have seldom declined food in my life). I enjoyed the thick hamburger she fried as I ate at the dining room table amidst documents of her eldest son's life, while she ate by the TV in the living room. I experienced various mixed messages from my hostess, who was very quick to respond to anything I expressed verbally as well as nonverbally. When I looked at the picture she declared was the only one Jimmy had ever painted in his life, I felt that there was a lot of depression in it since there was a windswept look to it. Lillian quickly pointed out, "Look at the bright green over here."

She then said, "I shouldn't do this but here's a box of things relevant to Jimmy's early years that I took down from the attic last week. You can take a look at it while I'm taking this call coming from a newscaster in Australia." I sat down at the table and started taking out the most interesting materials. In his ninth grade notebook he unconsciously expressed some doubts about himself as he wrote of "welcoming fearfully all wholesome ideas and experiences," when he clearly meant to write "fearlessly." Most striking was when, in his Annapolis diary, the print suddenly reduced to half its size after references to the sadistic hazing he was suffering at the hands of northern bullies and having hurt himself to lessen the hazing he faced. The first injury might have been accidental, but the second self-inflicted injury was an indicator of Carter being self-defeating. My first thought was, "Do I want to vote for someone who has self-defeating tendencies?"

There was such a large amount of invaluable material in the diary that I asked Miss Lillian if I could take it to the drugstore to make photocopies. She said it could not leave the house, but she agreed I could take pictures of it, and she in fact left for quite a while. I took pictures of his workbooks and especially of the diary. In my interaction with Miss Lillian I was impressed with just how bright and intuitive a woman she was, but I also felt caught in a double bind. She both wanted me to stay and go, to share with me, but was also afraid to share. Not that these mixed feelings didn't make some sense given the fact that next week her son would be up for election and that the *National Enquirer* reporters who had asked about Jimmy's childhood were using it for an exposé. I assured her, as I had with Gloria, that I was a scholar and that whatever I wrote would not be for journalism, but would be published after the election for scholarly purposes. I left her home utterly exhausted and exhilarated at these remarkable psychohistorical materials I had gathered despite my ignorance of Southern mores and extreme anxiety. I also felt thankful to my analyst who in my session before leaving had helped me to understand that I was a Northern liberal and had all sorts of stereotypes regarding Southerners and very little understanding of their culture.

At my presentation about my trip at the Institute for Psychohistory, I felt energized and also struck by the fact that a brilliant psychohistorical colleague had misread some of my evidence because of his own prejudices against Southerners and perhaps due to his envy that I had these valuable materials. Besides being published in *The Journal of Psychohistory*, my article and four others were put together in a book: *Jimmy Carter and American Fantasy: Psychohistorical Explorations* (1977). The specialness of being published was marred in part for me by two things written on the flyleaf. The most offensive were the bolded words, "Our conclusion is that Jimmy Carter—for reasons of his own personality and the powerful emotional demands of the American Fantasy—is likely to lead us into a new war by 1979." This clearly was not my conclusion or that of the majority of the authors in this edited book, which I told Lloyd deMause (the book's editor) in no uncertain terms. He blamed this conclusion projected onto all the authors on the publisher, but I had very serious doubts about what his role was in this misstatement. The flyleaf also said that all of the authors voted for Carter. This was true in my case, but as a scholar and unaffiliated voter, I didn't want it announced. Despite my frustration with him, Lloyd deMause played a significant role in launching my career as a presidential psychobiographer and publishing some of my work.

As Jimmy Carter walked with his family down Pennsylvania Avenue after the inauguration I had high hopes for his presidency, but I was also haunted by the insights into his personality that I had gained as a result of interviewing family members and lots of individuals from his childhood, as well as studying his career as governor of Georgia. When in 1978 I found myself writing the chapter, "Jimmy Carter as a Self-Defeatist," my doubts about his effectiveness led me to drop the book project. I felt that he was like the pilot of an airplane and I was one of the passengers. It didn't seem right to write about his self-defeating tendencies and shake the confidence of my fellow passengers, the American people. Had this issue come up later in my career I would not have been deterred by it since clearly I overestimated any influence I might have had, and I felt that somehow I would be betraying the trust of Jimmy's mother and sister, who had welcomed me into their homes. Actually, I identified closely with Carter; I once had a dream that I was his psychoanalyst. Later, I came to think of him as the captain of a less vulnerable and steadier ocean liner on which my fellow Americans and I were passengers. This was a far more realistic analogy. While I did not write the book on Carter, I did subsequently teach and give professional presentations on him, as well as publish on him in terms of presidential denigration and his work as peacekeeper.[2] Ultimately, I admire Carter far more as a former president who worked to better mankind and who continued to probe his own childhood than as a president.

Several colleagues complimented me on my article, especially my having declared Carter to have a narcissistic personality. This, however, was something I was very uncomfortable about for several reasons. To start with, anyone who runs for president is bound to have quite a lot of narcissism. More importantly, I remembered exactly why as an insecure psychohistorian I had declared him to have a "narcissistic personality with obsessive compulsive defenses." I remembered precisely sitting in an analytic class on narcissism and borderline phenomenon and feeling that I needed to have a psychoanalytic label to be taken seriously. The labeling was a reflection of my insecurity. I subsequently have worked extremely hard to avoid using psychiatric labels in my work. I maintained a correspondence with Gloria Carter and to a lesser extent with Lillian. Jimmy's sister said it felt very strange to read their words in my chapter, but in fact they were their words, and she granted me a much longer interview in 1977. She also reported that she gave the book to her brother and that he read it.

Throughout our history, presidents have been idealized or denigrated, but not systematically studied with great psychological insight until the 1970s. It was the presidency of Richard Milhous Nixon (1968–1974) that really launched the field of presidential psychobiography. Our thirty-seventh President's ethical lapses, near impeachment, and self-defeating inclinations led to a number of psychoanalytic studies. Psychiatrist and psychoanalyst David Abrahamsen was sought out by a publisher to write the valuable *Nixon vs. Nixon: An Emotional Tragedy* (1976). The UCLA historian Fawn Brody's *Richard Nixon: The Shaping of His Character* (1981) is a valuable study that was severely criticized for the author's honesty in acknowledging her strong anti-Nixon countertransference feelings. It is far more valuable than Bruce Mazlish's 1972 study, although I must credit it for getting me to think that a psychobiography of a sitting president could be done.[3]

As I avidly followed every presidential campaign, despite my best efforts to keep away from presidential psychobiography, I found the genre almost irresistible. After dropping the Carter book, I returned to English history, exploring the relationship between childhood and creativity among the entrepreneurs, innovators, and inventors of the Industrial Revolution of the second half of the eighteenth and early nineteenth centuries. However, I simply could not get much material on the subject for more than a few of the ninety-two individuals I was studying. Even when there was material, little of it was on their childhoods and not enough was on their personalities. In sharp contrast, modern presidential candidates have an enormous amount of personal childhood materials made available during their campaigns, which was part of the allure of the genre for me. When a colleague at an IPA meeting presented a very humorous paper on George H.W. Bush as having been depicted as a wimp and then becoming president, I teamed up with him, focusing on childhood and personality materials. I was able to arrange for the publication of our combined chapter, "George Bush: From Wimp to President" in a book that some analyst friends were publishing.[4] My co-author taught me the value of outlining before researching and writing. By his actions, he also taught me the dangers of quickly jumping to conclusions before carefully researching the sources. When I delved into Bush's early childhood I found the personality patterns that enabled him to become the first vice president since Martin Van Buren in 1837 to be elected directly from being second in command to being commander in chief. Presidents (and the public) are inclined to be very ambivalent about the man who benefits from their death in office and who may represent the unconscious, disclaimed death wish of the public to their leader. As a very young second son, Bush was nicknamed "have-half" because even on his birthday he was willing to accept an equal position with his older brother in the use of his new toy, since he accepted his older brother's dominance. While growing up, "have-half" maintained excellent relations with his brother, who he eventually displaced as the family hero.[5] In the White House when Reagan was shot, Vice President Bush demonstrated the ability to temporarily take over for President Reagan while convincing everyone of his loyalty to the man who had been his political rival. This heartfelt loyalty contrasted markedly with Secretary of State Alexander Haig's power drive leading him to say, "I am in control now!" Haig lost the confidence of the President and resigned the following year, while Bush's loyalty led to his being supported as Reagan's successor despite concerns that he was not a "true conservative."

As a presidential psychobiographer, I really came into my own in the 1992 election when I published "Psychobiographical Explorations of Clinton and Perot" with Herbert Barry, a colleague from whom I've learned quite a bit about sibling relationships.[6] A second 1992 psychobiographical article was "Character, Cancer, and Economic Regeneration in the 1992 campaign of Paul E. Tsongas."[7] Senator Tsongas (1941–1997) of Massachusetts had an openness and desire to talk to people and a concern for the economy that I greatly respected. However, a dilemma I had as a voter was the question of whether his cancer would return. Would I vote for him despite the fact that he might not be in good health or even live for four or eight years of a presidency? While he was my preferred candidate, I was saved from having to make that decision by his withdrawal from the Democratic primary race after he realized he was spending his daughter's money for college. Although he and his doctors were extremely optimistic about his cancer, in fact this admirable man would not have lived to serve as president for eight years. My experience with Tsongas led me to question if I should vote for the candidate I most admire, or for the one who appears to have the greatest likelihood of serving the country effectively.

While I like working with colleagues on projects, I came to see that co-authorship resulted in publications that I wasn't totally satisfied with. My voice was diluted and I simply didn't agree with everything that went out under my name. Eventually, the way I found to work closely with others without the reader being confused as to just what was my work was to do dialogues instead of co-authoring. This approach has been much more comfortable for me and I have done it mostly with Ken Fuchsman, who recently retired from the University of Connecticut.

William Jefferson Clinton was a psychohistorian's "gift that never stopped giving," though there were certainly moments when I certainly wished it would. My empathy for him remained strong when severe criticism of him in his first year or so of his presidency did not relent, even as he mourned the loss of his mother. This helped me to understand more of the issues regarding the denigration of presidents, which I had become much more aware of toward the end of Reagan's term and during George H.W. Bush's presidency. During the 1992 campaign, Clinton's mother spoke about the ability that she and her oldest son had to forget—I would say dissociate from—unpleasant realities. This trait haunted Bill Clinton and led to his impeachment at the hands of his political enemies since he seemed to really believe that he "did not have sex with that woman."[8]

While I only wrote about Reagan in passing, I learned a lot about the President's relationship with the public and the media and voters from the "Teflon President." How presidents managed national emotions during crises became a special interest of mine, and I admired Reagan's political skills, but not his morality, when he deflected public attention from the explosion that killed two-hundred and forty-one Marines in Lebanon by going to war in Granada to save U.S. medical students who, in fact, were not really in danger. This was in such sharp contrast to Carter's handling of the Iran Hostage Crisis, which he kept exacerbating because of the guilt he felt over being responsible for it. During the Reagan period I was working on historical dreams, which was a nice diversion from politics, although I was always on the lookout for dreams of presidents and presidential candidates. I trained as a dream researcher under Montague Ullman and subsequently developed a methodology for probing the dreams of historical personalities. In fact, it was a way of helping biographers to understand their own projections onto the deceased person and to greatly increase the possible interpretations of the dreams.

By the 1996 election, I decided that the best way I could write about the contenders without pathologizing was to do comparative studies.[9] In studying the Senate Majority Leader Bob Dole's unsuccessful bid for presidency, I was especially interested in his mechanisms of defense and how he overcame his devastating war injuries. This was reflected in the article "Work, Laughter, and Tears: Bob Dole's Childhood, War Injury, and Conservative Republicans in the 1996 Election." In the 1990s I found and was pleased that some foreign journals in Japan and Spain were republishing my presidential psychobiographies.

My comparative studies of presidential candidates became the staple of my presidential psychobiographies. The sharply contrasting personalities and values of candidates Al Gore and George W. Bush in 2000 were revealing. Each had recorded nightmares they dealt with differently. As a seven-year-old child shortly after the death of his little sister, "Little George" had repeated nightmares, his only recorded dream I could find. The family was torn by grief, yet failed to effectively mourn their beloved three-year-old, not even burying her at the time. Their eldest son became the family clown, and shared their denial of loss, even thinking he saw his sister after her death. Ultimately, I connected Bush's denial of "many of his feelings, choosing action over contemplation, which predisposed him to wage two ill-considered and ill-planned wars in his administration."[10] As a young congressman, Gore realized that he had answered a high school girl's question on nuclear proliferation with clichés, and then dreamt of a nuclear explosion as he huddled with his family. This led him to become more knowledgeable and proactive about nuclear issues. George W. Bush's war of choice in Iraq led me to write a symposium piece in 2003 in *Clio's Psyche* on teaching about the war, which was later reprinted in *The Journal of Psychohistory* as "Teaching about Bush's War in 21st Century America." Even before the war occurred, it was apparent from my study of the younger Bush's personality and values that he was motivated by personal considerations, as he wanted to both punish the Iraqi leader for an alleged plot to assassinate his father that the dictator was said to be behind and unconsciously to prove himself more successful than his father in fighting Saddam Hussein.

Researching Barack Obama's childhood helped me to understand how a biracial American (seen as a black man) could be elected president and the implications of this for his handling of the presidency. As a child in Indonesia when other children mocked him as black and literally threw stones at him, his mother taught him to ignore the insults and sidestep the rocks. He would be elected as a safe black man—a reconciler—but when the public wanted him to express their anger during the Great Recession of 2008, they discovered that this was not a ready part of his repertoire. The Republican leadership also discovered that it was safe to resist him since he mostly ignored the political rocks they threw at him without using the punitive powers of the presidency against them. The power of unrealistic savior fantasies that helped Obama win with a large majority in 2008, as well as be awarded a 2009 Nobel Peace Prize before he had time to achieve anything, resulted in millions being disappointed because their unrealistic fantasies were not fulfilled.

In 2016, while my main focus was on a comparison of Hillary Clinton and Trump, it was Trump who became the gift that kept on giving to the media and psychobiographers alike. Trump provided a new dilemma to me as the presidential psychobiographer with a strong desire to avoid pathologizing subjects. I had gotten around that problem at some other points by suggesting psychological concepts and insights but without using labels. In this way, I brought in the issue of superego lacuna in helping to explain Bill Clinton's ability to conveniently forget things that were distasteful. In the discussion of Trump, two factors were at work, making it more difficult to avoid psychological terminology. First and foremost, psychological terms were becoming so much more commonplace in the vocabulary of ordinary Americans. I, who had trained for eight years in psychoanalysis and had practiced it for a quarter century, avoided using pathological terms while I was listening to and reading laypeople using these terms. Second, as I read Trump's first book, *Trump: The Art of the Deal* (1987), he embraced his narcissism as a positive attribute of successful individuals and went on to refer to innovators perceived to be on the verge of lunacy as narcissistic and attributed this characteristic to himself. Trump said so many things and then disclaimed them, sometimes in the same sentence, that it seems strange to me to be avoiding pathologizing when he's wildly using projection all over the place.

Early on in my study, based on his campaign speeches and Twitter rants, I decided he was a case study in the coping mechanism of projection. Thus, whenever he denigrated someone else, I thought about those denigrations in terms of his own characteristics and usually it made lots of sense. Donald Trump created another predicament. In previously teaching and writing about presidential candidates, I had scrupulously avoided revealing my preferences. However, Trump was so unqualified for the presidency by virtue of his temperament and lack of governmental experience that I felt compelled to express my preferences to my students and in writing "A Presidential Psychobiographer's Countertransference to Trump."[11] In the year and a half since Trump was elected it is apparent that my fears that Trump's deficiencies in knowledge, preparation, probity, and temperament were well founded, and the country is floundering as a result.

Of course, my contributions to the field of presidential psychobiography must be examined in the context of what others have done. As early as 1912 a psychiatrist and follower of Freud, Morton Prince, published the article, "Roosevelt as Analyzed by the New Psychology," in the *New York Times* magazine. Leon Pierce Clark, a neurologist and psychoanalyst, wrote psychobiography and psychohistory on a regular basis in the 1920s and published a psychobiography of Lincoln in 1933, the year Clark died. Sigmund Freud and William Bullitt wrote a seriously flawed book, *Woodrow Wilson: A Psychological Study* (1966), on a man they each disliked intensely. Although historians and others complained about it,[12] *Woodrow Wilson and Colonel House: A Personality Study* (1964) by Alexander and Juliette George set a high standard of insight and only provided psychological terms in the Research Note in an afterward. Nixon and Clinton were sufficiently controversial so that, despite the Goldwater Rule of 1964, psychologically trained authors came forward to write on them and after Carter all presidents have had psychobiographical studies written about them. They are usually pathological studies, typically by psychologists, psychiatrists, and/or psychoanalysts without much background in studying presidents or considering the ethical issues involved. Justin Frank, trained at Harvard in psychiatry, is a professor at George Washington University Medical Center and a psychoanalyst who decided that without much research he could treat George W. Bush as a patient and write *Bush on the Couch: Inside the Mind of a President* (2004). His pathological study sold well enough for him to write *Obama on the Couch* (2011) and he is currently writing *Trump on the Couch*. To my mind, this type of study gives political psychobiography a bad name. Fidel Castro is reported to have extensively quoted the Bush book in his annual speech in 2004. For those contemplating writing presidential psychobiography, I recommend reading Stanley Renshon's book on the subject to help avoid writing an overtly pathological and unfounded study.[13]

Writing about a political leader whom you passionately think is taking your country in the wrong direction creates a serious dilemma for the political psychobiographer. Richard Nixon, whom I grew up detesting because he was a Red-baiting cold warrior, and also because of his policies of extending the war in Vietnam and bombing Cambodia, created a special problem. I found that I could use empathy to enable me to feel for ten-year-old Dick Nixon who missed his mother who was away, vainly trying to nurse an older brother back to health in Arizona. I felt for the lonely boy signing a letter to her, "your good dog Richard." I probed my own anger, fears, and narcissism to gain insight into these characteristics of Nixon.[14] In short, I used the tool of empathy to better understand our former president and curb my own biases as I wrote about him.

In 1976 I was certainly not alone in doing a psychohistorical study of Carter, who was unusually open and introspective for a politician. Bruce Mazlish joined with a journalist to write on him. The pair abided by the Goldwater Rule by interviewing the candidate, but had to endorse him for election as the price for getting an interview. They did this despite clearly having reservations about a religious fundamentalist who had been elected governor as a racist.[15] The greatest harm of the Goldwater Rule is the suppression of scholarship. It forces scholars to become advocates of candidates they may not believe in solely to get the required interview and permission to publish.[16]

Much of the presidential psychohistory scholarship was published in this period of the late 1970s in the aftermath of Nixon. Some of the best and most active authors of this time were David Beisel, Lloyd deMause, Betty Glad, and John Hartman. The young Doris Kearns Goodwin wrote her only explicitly psychohistorical book, *Lyndon Johnson and the American Dream* (1977), based on four years of intense personal weekend and vacation interviews of the former president at his ranch in Texas. In dealing with Johnson's grandiosity, regressions, and often lack of respect for personal boundaries, the young scholar had a unique support system at Harvard, which included Erik Erikson and the Group for Applied Psychoanalysis. She had, in effect, the equivalent of psychoanalytic supervision as she struggled with her own feelings toward a president whose reelection she had specifically opposed and with whom she formed an "intimate friendship."

Researching and writing candidate and presidential psychobiographies for over four decades has been quite an adventure that is a good test of my skills as a psychohistorian. My very uncertain start on Carter in 1976 has been followed by much more confident work on presidents and candidates, including the Bushes, the Clintons, Ross Perot, Paul Tsongas, Bob Dole, Richard Nixon, John Kerry, John McCain, Barack Obama, Mitt Romney, and Donald Trump. In the process, I developed a non-pathological approach focused on the family background, childhood, coping mechanisms, empathy, personality, style of leadership, and values. Because potential candidates start jockeying for position before the new president is inaugurated, this is a most time-consuming endeavor. More than once I have protested that I would not be doing this work in the next election, but in fact I find it to be addicting. The 2020 election is not that far off as I watch various governors and senators build their resumes. I suspect I will again find it to be irresistible, since I have often found my voice as a presidential psychobiographer.

Notes

1   On April 9, 2017 the letter appeared on the printed copy on page 26A.
2   "Presidential Responses to National Trauma: Case Studies of G.W. Bush, Carter, and Nixon," *The Journal of Psychohistory*, Vol. 36 (Summer 2008): pp. 36–58; "Presidents Carter and Sadat: The Repudiation of the Peacemakers," in Joan Zuckerberg, ed., *Politics and Psychology: Contemporary Psychodynamic Approaches* (New York: Plenum Press, 1991): pp. 143–173 (with Professor Mohammed Shalaan [Al Azhar University]).
3   *In Search of Richard Nixon: A Psychohistorical Inquiry* (1972).
4   Joan and Richard Zuckerberg, eds., *Politics and Psychology: Contemporary Psychodynamic Approaches* (New York: Plenum Press, 1991).
5   "Have-half" was a nickname that Bush outgrew and he is still known as "Poppy" within the family, which reflects an identification with his maternal grandfather. At birth his older brother Prescott's eye was injured, which restricted his success in school and sports, leading the family to look to George as the high achiever.
6   *The Journal of Psychohistory*, Vol. 20 (Fall 1992): pp. 197–216 (co-authored with Prof. Herbert Barry III of the University of Pittsburgh).
7   *The Journal of Psychohistory*, Vol. 20 (Fall 1992): pp. 217–227.
8   Paul H. Elovitz, "Clinton's 'Blind Spots' and 'The Rorschach Presidency,'" *Clio's Psyche*, Vol. 5 No. 3 (December 1998): pp. 69–77. This was one of twenty-three pieces on the subject of Clinton, Starr, Lewinsky, and impeachment.
9   "Clinton and Dole: A Psychohistorical Comparison," *Psychohistory News*, Vol. 16 (Fall 1996): pp. 1–4 and "Work, Laughter and Tears: Bob Dole's Childhood, War Injury, the Conservative Republicans and the 1996 Election," *The Journal of Psychohistory*, Vol. 24 (Fall 1996): pp. 147–162.
10 Paul H. Elovitz, "Grief and Loss of a Loved One in the Bush Family," *Clio's Psyche*, Vol. 15 No. 3 (December 2008): p. 118.
11 *Clio's Psyche*, Vol. 23 No. 1 (Fall 2016): pp. 1–8.
12 My friend, the psychoanalyst and psychologist James William Anderson, writes "the George and George study is an example of poor psychobiography, because their

research on Wilson's early life was abysmal." August 30, 2017 email from Anderson to me. Despite its imperfections, *Woodrow Wilson and Colonel House* inspired me and I continue to see its merits.

13 Stanley Renshon, *The Psychological Assessment of Presidential Candidates* (1996). Renshon, who is a psychoanalytically trained political scientist, has written about fifteen books including *High Hopes: The Clinton Presidency and the Politics of Ambition* (1996); *In his Father's Shadow: The Transformations of George W. Bush* (2004); (edited with Peter Suedfeld) *Understanding the Bush Doctrine: Psychology and Strategy in an Age of Terrorism* (2007); and *Barack Obama and the Politics of Redemption* (2012).

14 "Richard Milhous Nixon Revisited: The Haldeman Diaries," *The Psychohistory Review*, Vol. 24 (Winter 1995): pp. 99–111. I sent two versions of this article to the editors, one with my countertransference feelings based upon my family history and values and the other without it. I always regretted that they chose to publish the latter.

15 Bruce Mazlish and Edwin Diamond, "Thrice-Born: A Psychohistory of Jimmy Carter's 'Rebirth,'" *New York Magazine* (August 30, 1976).

16 In practice, candidates for the presidency, even if open to psychohistory, have not wanted to risk having psychohistorians interview them because our findings can so easily be taken out of context and used by opponents in smear campaigns.

12

FINDING MY VOICE WITH HALPERN, DEMAUSE, AND ULLMAN

Three colleagues who have enormously influenced my thinking and writing are Sidney Halpern, Lloyd deMause, and Montague Ullman. The influence of each has been powerful, yet very different. I became a historian to find out about my father's past and what lay behind the lies my normally very honest parents told me.[1] Becoming a psychoanalytically trained psychohistorian enabled me to delve much more deeply into my family history and myself. In the process of doing this I discovered I had a loud and clear voice.

When I was a very small boy, only my mother and year-and-a-half older sister could understand what I said. By the time I went to kindergarten, which a teacher recommended I repeat because of my immaturity and shyness,[2] people understood me, but through much of my life I have feared not being understood. Finding my literary voice was also not easy. My first recollection of writing is being unable to do it. The situation was that my mother told me to write a letter to my grandfather in Minnesota, whom I did not know, but I knew my father disliked because Grandpa Harry was a communist more concerned with saving the world than in taking proper care of his family. Mom finally told me what to write. Thereafter, whenever I had to write something, I would procrastinate and then finally write in a rush out of fear of failing.

Childhood memories of listening to accounts of my father's life as an Eastern European Jew influenced my choice of history as my profession. When friends visited him, my father sometimes told stories, often in a language I did not understand, of his adventures in the Russian Civil War. Whenever possible, I eavesdropped on these conversations with rapt attention. I loved the adventure of history and had no conflicts about it. However, as I grew older and I asked Dad about his experiences in Europe, he clammed up, wanting me to focus on other things. He hoped I would become a medical doctor, not a historian. But the seed had already been planted, even though it did not germinate until after I served in the Army and needed to decide on a career.

It was during my time in the Army that my mother died after four years of struggling with cancer. I came home from Germany on emergency leave to sit by her bedside for over a week as she prepared to die from the cancer that had destroyed her body. After my mother's death when she was fifty and I was twenty-two, Dad dropped hints about her life as a communist organizer prior to their living together and marriage. However, he discouraged my questions and even gave me false information to keep me from researching her front-page role as "Red Rose," which had resulted in her being jailed for two to four months. She had organized a May demonstration for free meals for school children and unemployed workers during the Great Depression.[3] Mom became a liberal Democrat who was disillusioned by her jailing and never spoke of her early political activities to her children.

As a very small boy I was terrified by the rats running on the metal ceiling overhead, our apartment being burglarized, my sister being sexually abused, the numerous vagrants on the street, and mostly frightening images as I tried to fall asleep. Mom calmed me by drawing an image of a perfect world of peace and happiness.[4] A legacy of my early fear is a lifelong inability to literally see visual images with my eyes closed except when asleep. To me, Mom represented the dream of a utopian world, and Dad stood for a hardheaded questioning approach to people's motivations and leaders in particular. Both had a strong influence on me and how I have conducted my life. It is unfortunate that I never knew Mom when I was an adult, rather than as a son trying to establish my own personality and life plan, as I knew Dad in his last decade.

My life patterns were set by my parents, but strongly influenced by the three men discussed below.

My colleague Professor Sidney Halpern at Temple University opened the interrelated worlds of psychoanalysis and psychohistory to me and helped me work through my dissertation writer's block. He was a self-made man, like my father, a trait I admired enormously. This brilliant intellectual was an ancient historian, contrarian, and much, much more. He had founded an insurance company, which had a hundred employees and a thousand agents when he left it to become a modestly paid college teacher. He had some psychoanalytic training he dropped out of because he wanted to directly improve the lives of his patients. Analytic distance was never his forte. Halpern threw himself into whatever he did, including helping friends like me. At one point, he was publisher of Mercury Books and on the Editorial Board of *American Imago*, as well as its business manager. Sid did not write much and what he did write he was inclined to keep as a mystery from me, although I did find his article arguing that Socrates, as portrayed in Aristophanes's play *The Clouds*, was the first psychoanalyst, since Socrates answered a question with a question.[5] In just a few years, I learned to think psychohistorically by auditing his classes, reading the books he recommended, and especially in discussion with him.

One of my last acts as a faculty member at the Ambler Campus was to sit on a small committee that successfully recommended Sid to become director of the campus. In a few years, he transformed the sleepy six hundred-student Ambler into a full-fledged extension campus of almost seven thousand young people in overflowing classes. Fear of crime and ethnic white flight from Philadelphia caused Ambler to prosper under his dynamic leadership, but these movements also meant large-scale de-tenuring at the downtown campus. In a short period of time, the history department lost thirty of its eighty-three members. Regrettably, despite telling me that he would not accept the college president's offer of becoming dean in charge of confronting the fiscal crisis, what he called becoming the "hatchet man," he soon did just that, helping to save Temple from bankruptcy and I am sure leading many colleagues to despise him.

After I moved to Northern New Jersey, we kept in touch despite the distance, and I occasionally visited him. Sid continued to advise me when, as a psychological historian, I had to fight for my job at Ramapo and listened when I vented about difficulties in dealing with Lloyd deMause, who wanted disciples more than colleagues. As I look back on our relationship, I remember having serious doubts about some things that he did, but I was too much in awe of him to voice my concerns. However, I had no trouble rejecting many of his values as not my own. For example, Sid was a political conservative, a supporter of the war in Vietnam, and a Jewish chauvinist, and I rejected all of those positions while remaining a proud Jew and continuing to protest the war in Vietnam. After a few years I was shocked by what was happening with Sidney Halpern. He became severely depressed and his health deteriorated to the point where he declared himself to be "ill, iller, illest, and brain dead."[6] Although he had once picketed Nixon's White House over an issue involving Israel, he came to see Richard Nixon during Watergate as a Christ-like martyr. At moments he acted outrageously, as when he flunked all of his students in an advanced course, de-tenured his ex-wife whom he had helped get a professorship at Temple, and lost all of his money, so despite his terrible health he had to keep teaching to have money to live on.[7] I wondered how such a brilliant and generous man could act so badly and even self-destructively. Clearly, the limited psychoanalysis he had was no magic solution to his problems. My feelings for Sid remain dominated by gratitude and sadness. Upon his death I established the Sidney Halpern Award for the "Best Idea in an Article or Book on Psychohistory."[8]

Intellectuals with sweeping explanations had a strong appeal for me in my early years. The great twentieth-century intellectual Sir Isaiah Berlin (1909–1997) made a distinction between thinkers who were like hedgehogs and foxes. Hedgehogs sit on their mounds seeing for miles in all directions coming up with a single idea, and foxes sniff around following specific sights and smells. Thinkers like Karl

Marx, with his sweeping generalizations about classes, is a hedgehog, while most intellectuals know many different topics well, thus they are foxes. According to this generalization, I am a fox who started with an awe of hedgehogs. In listening to myself in psychoanalysis, I eventually came to distrust idealization generally and sweeping explanations in history.

Lloyd deMause initially had strong appeal to me as an intellectual hedgehog, a self-made entrepreneur like Halpern and my father, and a psychohistorical leader and editor. In just a few years, he built a thriving psychohistorical community, which published a journal, wrote books, created an international organization with annual conventions, and had meetings in alternate months in the imposing conference room of his Broadway business. I was learning constantly, including from the content presented at the Institute for Psychohistory Saturday meetings, of which I was co-founder and the chief organizer. Every year there was a cocktail party in Lloyd's fourteenth-floor Riverside Drive condominium overlooking the Hudson River, at which I got to know some wonderful contributors to our field.[9]

As I probed my own childhood in my analysis, Lloyd deMause's heavily foot-noted "Evolution of Childhood" essay filled in a part of history that graduate school wasn't teaching. I read it with great enthusiasm and was inspired to offer a course on children in history, as well as to find out everything I could about the childhood of everyone I studied. It seemed extraordinary that deMause was raising his son Neil in what he labeled "helping mode parenting," based on the premise "that the child knows better than the parent what it needs at each stage of its life" and the parent neither disciplines nor attempts to form "habits" in the homeschooled child. The parent essentially becomes a servant to the child. It eventually seemed to me to be a utopian upbringing, which he said resulted "in a child who is gentle, sincere, never depressed, never imitative or group-oriented, strong willed, and unintimidated by authority."[10] I shook my head in amazement at the commitment of time and energy Lloyd deMause devoted to his son and wondered what this parenting meant for his wife and son.

Lloyd's categorization of childhood into six modes had always seemed too formulaic to me, and I came to believe that his helping mode parenting was an ideal, not a reality, and perhaps not such a good idea. It certainly seemed impracti-cal to make the parent the servant of the child. In my experience, those parents who talked in similar terms were permissive to the point that their children did not have any structure. Despite deMause's idealization of what he calls "helping mode parenting," I found that kids are much better off with consistency, even if it does involve light spanking. Doing therapy with families and children also led to my questioning the advisability of aiming for helping mode childrearing. Further-more, Lloyd's first wife had left the family and tragically died while walking on a road in the Southwest.[11] On one occasion Lloyd, who appeared to be in analysis probing his own life and behavior most of the time, said that he had slipped and hit his son on five occasions. I began to wonder whether in trying so hard to not repeat the pattern of an abusive father who had razor strapped him, he had simply gone too far in the other direction.

Amidst all these new ideas and behaviors, dark clouds soon began to appear. Henry Ebel, the man closest to deMause in those early years, was a brilliant and erratic Holocaust survivor whose inappropriate poetry appeared in *The Journal of Psychohistory*. One night we found ourselves waiting in the lobby of a hospital since Henry had had a dangerous delusional reaction to LSD. I thought it outrageous that a stimulating meeting had been ruined by one person's behavior, but I did not feel confident enough to open my mouth in protest. So instead, I soon went home with a bitter taste in my mouth, wondering why we had followed deMause to the emergency room. Lloyd deMause started *Behavior Today* for Ebel to have a job editing, but it did not last long. Henry's wife divorced him after their toddler ingested some LSD that he had left in the refrigerator.[12]

DeMause had what seemed to be a wonderful idea of making our groups self-analytic on the grounds that this would protect the groups from making bad choices. Group self-analysis can be extremely helpful when done skillfully, as it was at the first IPA meetings in 1978 with John J. Hartman, who had studied group process at Harvard.[13] However, it can be disastrous for a group when mishandled. The latter was the case when Glenn Davis, who had only attended a lengthy Institute meeting for a few minutes, wrote up group process notes that were sent out to participants and others. His analysis named participants and had everything to do with deMause's theories and little to do with what actually occurred. I suspected that what he wrote was based on Lloyd deMause discussing the meeting with him. I strongly protested the distribution of these minutes by Henry Lawton as detrimental to the group's functioning and he ceased doing it.[14]

Group process analysis became a mainstay of the IPA, for better and worse, mostly depending on the skill of the group process analysts. Except for the very successful first conference's sessions at the end of each day, it was mostly worse in the early years. A basic problem was that some participants were analyzed, some being psychoanalysts, and others were not. Some understood the workings of the unconscious and how to protect the confidentiality and feelings of others, and others used group process sessions as a place for wild analysis. One year Casper Schmidt and Lloyd, as group process analysts, in a very authoritarian manner, declared what others were feeling, regardless of what others were actually thinking and feeling. A person who came a great distance at great expense to attend exciting meetings said it would be nice to have a welcoming committee at the convention, only to be told by Schmidt: "YOU WANT TO BE FED!" This was repeated several times as the bewildered and offended person making the suggestion protested that this was not the case. On a more positive note, Howard F. Stein was inspired by Hartman's group process to study groups, became a group consultant, and became an excellent IPA group analyst. I struggled to make group process work for about seven or eight years and then in frustration gave up on it, only at times to be pleasantly surprised by its success. Overall, it drove far more people away than it attracted, and it badly hurt the IPA's reputation.

Extremely important studies were being presented at the IPA, the Institute for Psychohistory, and printed in the pages of *The Journal of Psychohistory*, which, despite the general misconception to the contrary, had no legal connection to the IPA.[15] Exciting new ideas were being probed and debated at our meetings with mixed results. In the Independence of Psychohistory Symposium's lead article, Lloyd deMause put forth his revolutionary view that psychohistory is a science "specifically concerned with establishing laws and discovering causes."[16] To him psychohistorians were like astronomers, and he compared historians to astrologers. Barbara Tuchman, the Pulitzer Prize-winning popular historian, said that deMause spoiled his argument when he made the "unconvincing overstatement about 100 historians giving 1% of their space to motivation" since "motivation cannot be separated from events."[17] When deMause complained that he devoted two million dollars of his own money to getting academics to subscribe or renew their subscriptions to the journal, he readily dissociated from statements like this that were so insulting to the people he was courting.[18] While I briefly considered the idea of psychohistory being a science rather than an art, I quietly rejected it. To me, psychohistory is an art which uses the scientific method whenever possible to get at the truth.[19]

Lloyd deMause always had a strong interest in birth and published what others wrote about it before coming forth with the "fetal origins of history." He introduced it with his usual disclaimers along the lines of "this will shock you and you will think it is crazy, but my research shows that . . ." It did shock colleagues. For example, three talented historians from Boston, Martin Quitt, Richard Lyman, and Patrick Dunn, who regularly drove down to New York to our meetings in Manhattan in a Volkswagen Beetle, drove home, according to what Marty told David Beisel, laughing all the way about the nonsense of the fetal origins of history. They all left the IPA, with the immediate impact being the loss of the newsletter editors. The medieval historian Richard Lyman of this group told me that he was especially worried that association with deMause would hurt his academic career. Marty and Dick had done a fine job as IPA newsletter editors, reflecting the interests of and showing a sensibility to the historical profession. Henry Lawton, as a diligent independent scholar, simply did not have this sensibility when he took over as editor.

Another negative turning point was when Howard Stein, a former Yeshiva student then in rebellion against his religion, published "Judaism and the Group Fantasy of Martyrdom: The Psychodynamic Paradox of Survival through Persecution,"[20] in the Judaism as a Group Fantasy Special Issue. This was and is certainly a sensitive subject in the shadow of the Holocaust that had killed a third of all Jews. However, the way the materials were presented was a significant part of the problem. As an editor who has often published controversial and emotional subjects, I think the crucial issue is how materials are presented. Lloyd deMause followed his typical approach, aiming for shock value. Many scholars and clinicians were shocked and some determined to never have anything to do with deMause and those associated with him, which many generalized into New York psychohistorians. Accordingly, the *Journal*, the IPA, the Institute, and psychohistory generally suffered a body blow to their reputations.

Fantasy analysis is a theory that deMause developed early on to gauge the emotional life of the nation in relation to the Reagan presidency and asked for volunteers to form a fantasy analysis group, which met monthly in Manhattan. It was comprised of Casper Schmidt, Henry Lawton, Howard Stein (at a distance in Oklahoma), and me. Each of us looked at separate news sources. What deMause and Schmidt reported finding had little to do with what Lawton and I were finding. At our meeting before Hinckley attempted to assassinate Reagan on March 30, 1981, deMause and Schmidt noted that there were considerable violent images in the news; however, this was not uncommon and it was not what Lawton and I were reporting. Right after the assassination attempt, they declared that they had predicted it at our meeting. While they may have thought it or said it privately, neither Henry Lawton nor I heard it.

I thought Lloyd deMause's fantasy analysis methodology was promising, but that it needed major refinements and was too dependent on the unconscious of the researchers. Privately, I likened it to trying to do brain surgery with a butcher's knife rather than a scalpel. Although I personally did not find it very helpful, I brought two colleagues together and over a six month period organized a fantasy analysis project in which we looked for correlations among the fantasy analysis responses of colleagues to two documents.[21] Lloyd deMause seized our results as proof positive of the scientific basis of fantasy analysis, but I thought that our research sample was too small and too influenced by deMause's concepts to draw these conclusions. I then planned a quite scientific study with colleagues quite experienced in interpreting the unconscious, but I was unable to get the necessary funding for that project.

On the basis of his fantasy analysis work, Lloyd deMause was invited to Washington to give a Saturday talk to some of Reagan's staff on their theories regarding the emotional relationship of the public to the president.[22] At the end of the presentation, made with Casper, they inquired what the staff thought of their ideas. They were told, "We talk to everyone, next week we have a psychic coming to the White House." We eventually learned that it was the psychic, not the psychohistorians, who was listened to! It was a national disgrace that the astrologer influenced White House decisions, but privately I was glad that deMause did not because he was promising far more than psychohistory could deliver at the present stage of our knowledge.

Lloyd deMause was drawn to clearly brilliant, but erratic individuals such as Henry Ebel and later Casper Schmidt. Both liked to scandalize, which drove people away from our field. Casper Schmidt gave a professional presentation at the height of the AIDS crisis claiming that the etiology of the disease was purely psychological. At the time, my nephew was dying of this terrible disease and Casper himself later died of HIV/AIDS. DeMause seemed to be empowered by more radical thinkers who served as surrogates for his most radical notions. Glenn Davis was a third surrogate of deMause and a likable young political science graduate student who was not well grounded emotionally or as a scholar.

In the early 1980s, I remember chatting with the Hartford psychoanalyst Mel Goldstein about Lloyd deMause, who said to me, "You can't get blood from a stone," meaning that I wanted something from Lloyd that he could not give. Perhaps it was the approval of a parental figure. What Mel said stuck with me. I discussed it with my psychoanalyst, and I soon became much more realistic in dealing with Lloyd deMause and in what I expected from him.[23] In the period after this incident I became more willing to follow my own lights and listen to my own voice. In the 1980s, although deMause was opposed to it, I successfully supported the establishment of various awards, for which I raised much of the money, mostly to encourage graduate and undergraduate students in psychohistory.

Eventually at IPA meetings there was a mostly unspoken agreement among David Beisel, Mel Kalfus, and me to reign in Lloyd deMause when he behaved inappropriately. David refers to his "outrageous behavior," such as opening the door of a room full of attendees as Danielle Knafo was about to start her presentation and saying that he would be presenting in the next room, so virtually everyone got up and went to hear him talk. After a presentation, Lloyd often spoke immediately in the question and answer session, telling the audience and author about how the subject somehow fit into his theories. As chairs of the session, often self-designated when this situation arose, David, Mel, and I failed to recognize his hand until later in the discussion, and if he spoke anyway we would tell him to wait his turn. He always got his say, but we consciously fought his periodic inclination to make the IPA the International Lloyd deMause Association.

In the mid-1980s, although I was vice-president publically designated to be IPA president, I was blocked from the presidency. This caused a breech with my friend Henry Lawton, of whom I was unfailingly supportive. In a situation where one vote of the executive committee made the difference, he was too intimated by Lloyd and Casper to vote for me as president when I could not attend an officers meeting due to teaching obligations. I finally became president in 1988 in Washington, DC at the only IPA conference not held in New York City. When my luggage was misplaced on the flight to DC, I needed a dress shirt and Lloyd kindly offered me the use of one of his. It seemed somehow symbolic to me that I could not wear his shirt because his chest was much narrower than mine. Fortunately, the airline brought mine in time. My presidency went well, partly because I learned to ignore the inevitable second hand reports of deMause finding fault with one thing or another.

DeMause saw *The Emotional Life of Nations* (2002) as his magnum opus. At the request of Andrew Brink, a member of the Board of Editors of *Clio's Psyche*, I organized a symposium that eleven colleagues contributed to with Lloyd responding to at length.[24] To put it mildly, on the whole, the historians did not have a favorable view of the book and its scholarship. One Midwestern historian, who served on our Board of Editors, found so many historical mistakes in the first twenty or so pages that he refused to write for the symposium since he considered the book an embarrassment.

Early in the twenty-first century, out of the blue Lloyd muttered something to me, in a questioning manner to the effect, "They have to be wrong, I haven't hurt psychohistory." I felt sad for him and gave him a reassuring look. There is a tragic element to Lloyd's life devoted to building psychohistory while alienating so many interested colleagues.

Shortly after Obama was elected, Lloyd deMause asked me to write my usual presidential candidate political psychobiography of Hillary Clinton. I told him I would some years hence—and I did seven years later. Clearly, he was losing his sense of time. Denis O'Keefe had deMause speak to his NYU class, and then an hour later one of Denis's students found Lloyd wandering the street in a lost manner, so she drove him home. In 2014 at the IPA, there was a hastily put together luncheon honoring deMause, who had been brought there by his wife, Susan Hein. I was amazed that *only* two other colleagues who did not know him nearly as well spoke briefly about Lloyd's accomplishments,[25] so I spoke in a heartfelt way about the wonderful thing our founding president had done to bring so many colleagues together to do psychohistory and to provide a place to publish their work. I felt sadness for a man who had devoted his life to my field and who was unsure of his legacy—as well he might be. As he struggles with Alzheimer's disease, his wife reports that it is still psychohistory that he really cares about. Regrettably, he was so devoted to psychohistory that he did not focus on having sufficient retirement funds for his family and his later years, so Susan is forced to work hard at an age when she should be able to retire. Lloyd deMause seemed to never be able to say that he made money from psychohistory, which is perhaps why he put so much of his own money into advertising the *Journal*. There are elements of Greek tragedy in Lloyd deMause's relationship with psychohistory, a field he did so much to build while simultaneously hurt. It is hard for me to determine if he did more to help or hurt the field.

On several occasions when deMause had offended colleagues, it was quietly suggested that I use the Psychohistory Forum as a rival to the IPA. This I dismissed out of hand, since my idea was always to have a big tent approach to psychohistory, cooperating with Lloyd and everyone else to build our field. The question remains as to why I was so willing to work with deMause when his values and mine were so in conflict and when he had abruptly terminated the Saturday Workshops in 1982. The answer is multifaceted. Certainly, I have always been quite appreciative of what he did for psychohistory and he was a parental figure for me in the early years. Lloyd's dream of a better world through improved childrearing tied into the utopian impulse I learned from my mother. Publishing my political psychobiography and other articles in the *Journal* was something

I valued. In it, I could publish longer articles than in *Clio's Psyche* and include lots of footnotes. Finally, I had no desire to be a competitor to deMause, since this did not fit my personality, which left me more comfortable as a facilitator and nurturer of psychohistory than an organizational rival. For forty years I have attended the IPA, sharing my research with colleagues.[26] In fact, I serve on its planning committee as I continue to work to strengthen this organization.

There is appreciation and ambiguity in my feelings for Sidney Halpern and Lloyd deMause, but not for Montague Ullman (1916–2008).[27] Toward this dream group leader, psychoanalyst, psychiatrist, and pioneer dream laboratory researcher I feel only admiration, appreciation, and warmth. I heard Monte—everyone called him Monte—speak at my psychoanalytic training institute in 1982 and soon traveled to his home in Ardsley, New York to participate in his dream workshop and do dream group training. In psychoanalytic training, my dream interpretation course had been a disappointment and I had not been particularly successful in doing dream work with my patients. They looked to me for the understanding of their dreams while the answer was within them. Monte's technique kept the focus on the dreamer. He was such a wonderful and playful listener who had created a safe group structure that encouraged openness and sharing to an amazing degree. When it would help someone, he would share his own experiences. For example, I had a dream revealing considerable death anxiety as I approached the age at which my brother and mother had died. Monte spoke of his own anxiety when he had approached the age at which his father had died of a stroke. When a foreign physician arrived in our group acting like a bull in a china shop, Monte listened to his own dream in which the disrupter appeared as a teddy bear. In short order his dream was prophetic since the newcomer calmed down and became a cooperative member of the group. Our unconscious sees things our conscious is so often blind to.

Working with Ullman was such a pleasure that I found a reason to involve him in psychohistorical research. On a sabbatical in England in 1981, I discovered a treasure trove of dreams of the scientist Sir Humphry Davy (1778–1829) that I was struggling to understand. With the help of Don Hughes of Denver, Mena Potts of Ohio, and Ullman, I developed the Historical Dreamwork Method in which the historian role-plays the historical personage being probed.[28] A historian colleague and some psychoanalysts immediately protested, "Since you don't have a living dreamer to free associate how can you find out anything more about the meaning of the dream?"[29] What the method yielded was additional possible interpretations and helping the biographer understand what s/he was projecting onto the deceased dreamer. I was so excited about the dreams I was finding that I wrote various articles on the subject and half of the book, *The Creativity of Dreams*, which unfortunately I never found time to finish. While Ullman-style dream work was a wonderful way to help individuals understand their unconscious, it was a terrible way to earn enough money to pay the electric bill! However, it did benefit my teaching, since I went from role-playing historical dreamers to role-playing historical personages and events with my students. Ullman had developed the first dream laboratory under the most scientific of conditions. I used his approach as a model in proposing a research project on fantasy analysis, which unfortunately never received the necessary funding.

As an ego ideal of connectedness, humanity, intelligence, research methodology, warmth, and wit, Monte Ullman remains very much alive within me. Two external ways I have of reminding me of all that Monte stood for is to drink from a cup that had been his and to look at the pachysandra ground cover surrounding my home that I planted in emulation of the pachysandra he had planted by his walkway in Ardsley.

Together with my parents, these three men each had a profound influence on me and on the psychohistory I do. In different ways, they each helped me find my voice. Sidney Halpern introduced me to the field and got me started reading and thinking psychohistorically. Lloyd deMause brought me together with numerous colleagues and helped me realize my organizational skill in the Saturday Institute for Psychohistory meetings, as well as to give me a place to publish. In relationship to him I developed my own clear voice. Montague Ullman helped me to become a better listener and researcher, as well as to trust what was within me as revealed in my dreams and nightmares. I find disappointment in the latter years of the lives of Halpern and deMause and much happiness in Ullman's life. In his ninth decade, he was feeling so joyful that he told me that perhaps he should write the book, *Life Begins at Ninety*.

Notes

1 Paul H. Elovitz, "Family Secrets and Lies My Parents Told Me: The Impact of Immigrants on Their Son," in Paul H. Elovitz and Charlotte Kahn, eds., *Immigrant Experiences: Personal Narrative and Psychological Analysis* (1997): pp. 95–117.

2 When I researched the school records, the actual grades were not failing, just rather low. My mother, who was then in awe of teachers, followed this recommendation and had me repeat kindergarten. I felt humiliated by this, and at my mother's recommendation I took summer classes in high school to finish in three years in an attempt to not feel behind my age cohort. Despite graduating high school in three years and earning advanced degrees, until recent years I never saw myself as being smart.

3 The *Waterbury Democrat* and the *New York Times* gave contradictory information on her sentence. In the Spring 2018 issue of *Clio's Psyche*, I published "The Disillusionment of Red Rose" on her failed attempt to get a legal permit to demonstrate, her arrest, and the newspaper coverage of her disenchantment in jail.

4 At the time I did not know about the sexual abuse of my sister, but I knew about the fear my family felt in terms of the neighborhood.

5 Baruch Halpern, "Sidney Halpern (1927–1994): Memoir of a Psychohistorian," *Clio's Psyche*, Vol. 2 No.1 (June 1995): pp. 6–8.

6 Halpern, "Sidney Halpern," p. 7.

7 Because Sid lived modestly I am puzzled as to what happened to his money, beyond the half of it he might have had to surrender in the divorce to his wife, who was a lawyer. I suspect it was devoted to his health care costs.

8   The monetary funds that I collected from Halpern's family and colleagues have been exhausted, but the Psychohistory Forum has a used set of *The Complete Works of Sigmund Freud* that is available to be given as an award.

9   I have enjoyable recollections of chatting with historian George Kren (1926–2000), who looked like Leon Trotsky and was working to establish a psychohistory graduate program with his psychologist colleague Leon Rappoport at Kansas State University. Regrettably, the program was not successful and George, who always seemed to have a cigarette in his mouth, died of lung cancer.

10 Lloyd deMause, "The Evolution of Childhood," *The History of Childhood Quarterly: The Journal of Psychohistory*, Vol. 1 No. 4 (Spring 1974): pp. 554–556.

11 I wondered if she had felt overwhelmed by Lloyd's unusually intense involvement in parenting.

12 Mel Goldstein of the University of Hartford connected Henry Ebel to an administrative position at his institution, but felt betrayed when Henry misused for his own administrative purposes a grant of ten thousand dollars that Mel's son in business had arranged for his company to give to the University. David Beisel reports that Ebel was fired as a result of this malfeasance, although he was a graduate school friend of the university's president who later rehired him when he became president of George Washington University.

13 Alice Eichholz was Hartman's partner in this first, very successful, experiment with group process analysis. Eichholz was also co-founder with me of the Institute for Psychohistory's Saturday Seminar program. Hartman's main interpretation was that the attendees at the first IPA were like a Bar Mitzvah boy on his best behavior whose leather jacket and motorcycle were right outside the door. Some subsequent group process analyses were a very wild ride!

14 Henry gave the names and gist of what was said by each, which exacerbated the situation. I was horrified that Glenn Davis would write and send out group process notes about meetings of the Institute for Psychohistory that he only spent a few minutes at or never even attended. My assumption at the time was that he became a spokesman for Lloyd.

15 Many professional organizations provide a journal with membership, but this has never been the case with the IPA. The primary reason for this is that *The Journal of Psychohistory* makes a profit for Lloyd deMause and his family. Personally, as the editor of a small scholarly journal, I think it is wonderful that one publication in our field makes a profit.

16 "The Independence of Psychohistory," *The Journal of Psychohistory*, Vol. 3 No. 2 (Fall 1975): p. 164.

17 "Comment by Barbara Tuchman," *The Journal of Psychohistory*, Vol. 3 No. 2 (Fall 1975): p. 184.

18 Lloyd deMause, "My Reply to the Reviewers," *Clio's Psyche*, Vol. 10 No. 2 (September 2003): p. 53.

19 See my "Art and Science in Psychohistory," *Clio's Psyche*, Vol. 13 No. 1 (June 2006): pp. 11–13.

20 *The Journal of Psychohistory*, Vol. 6 No. 2 (Fall, 1978): pp. 151–210. Howard is the only member of our group who regularly wears a yarmulke to meetings.

21 "On Doing Fantasy Analysis," with Henry Lawton and George Luhrmann, *The Journal of Psychohistory*, Vol. 13 No. 2 (Fall 1985): pp. 207–228.

22 It is my impression that Mary Coleman, who with Carol Ravenal had established a very active Washington branch of the Institute for Psychohistory, made the connection to the White House staff.

23 There was a correlation with my expectations of Lloyd and of my father who could be very critical at times. In the last ten years of Dad's life, after I had a fair amount of psychoanalysis, I could easily short circuit his criticism and enjoy his warmth and

personality without interruptions. After I had smooth relations with Dad, it became easier to deal with Lloyd.

24 *The Emotional Life of Nations* Symposium, *Clio's Psyche*, Vol. 10 No. 2 (September 2003): pp. 33–55. Andrew Brink was a wonderful literary scholar whose idealization of deMause clouded his judgment.

25 One was Ludwig Janus, a German psychiatrist who has been working on the impact of our fetal past. Janus is a key leader of the German psychohistorical association.

26 At this point I take pride in being the only colleague who has attended and presented at every annual meeting of the IPA.

27 The "Ullman Memorial Dream Feature" of *Clio's Psyche* (Vol. 15 No. 2 [September 2008]: pp. 57, 77–86) contains eight memorial appreciations of this truly remarkable man.

28 "Psychohistorical Dreamwork: Section I," in Claire Limmer and Montague Ullman, eds., *The Variety of Dream Experience* (New York: Continuum Books, 1987).

29 I responded with my article, "Dreams as a Psychohistorical Source," *The Journal of Psychohistory*, Vol. 6 No. 3 (Winter 1989): pp. 289–296. My argument peaked the interest of the doubter, but it took attending a historical dream workshop to really convince those who questioned the method.

13

BUILDERS OF PSYCHOHISTORY

There are numerous colleagues who play or have played important roles in building psychohistory, aside from the ones mentioned in the previous comparative chapters. Those covered below do not represent comprehensive coverage of the builders. Those I have met and worked with are far better represented than those I have not known or had personal contact with. They are not listed according to the order of their contributions. Though some are grouped based on being psychiatrists/medical doctors, Holocaust survivors/researchers, academic psychologists, close associates of deMause, and so forth, most are not in any particular order. To view pictures of some of my psychohistorical colleagues, go to the *Clio's Psyche* website at cliospsyche.org. For me, it is partly a trip down memory lane.

It should be pointed out that most who research and write psychohistory do it for only a limited period of time.[1] Such is not the case with David Beisel, who has an outstanding record as a psychohistorical editor, educator, leader, and scholar. As a leader, he organized the first conference of the IPA with impressive competency and did the same a second time years later when called upon. When the Berlin conference fell through in the mid-1980s, he stepped in and at the last minute put together a conference in Manhattan. From 1980–1989 he edited *The Journal of Psychohistory*, setting up a refereeing system that unfortunately was not continued after he stepped down. He is a prolific author on a variety of subjects in American, European, and German history. His pathbreaking monograph, *The Suicidal Embrace: Hitler, the Allies, and the Origins of the Second World War* (2003), skillfully applied family therapy to the interwar diplomacy. Beisel, a lover of jazz, edited *Wounded Centuries: A Selection of Poems* (2016), the first book of psychohistorical poetry, because he knows that poetry, like music, has an amazing ability to express the unconscious. As an outstanding psychohistorical teacher, he has introduced eight thousand students to our field at SUNY-RCC. He brought his students to IPA meetings and in one case, a talented student, Denis O'Keefe, went on to become IPA president and is a fine young psychohistorian. As someone who worked quite effectively with deMause to build the IPA and psychohistory, Beisel grew increasingly frustrated by what deMause was doing to drive scholars and clinicians away from the field that he also did so much to build.

I met psychiatrist Chaim "Hi" Shatan (1924–2001) at the first IPA conference in 1978 and have fond memories of his warmth and empathy for the mothers of newborns in therapy with him. He would visit them in the hospital just after they gave birth. In terms of resistance to psychological approaches, Chaim suggested that half the time when a word begins with "psycho," the listener tunes the content out because the unspoken question becomes, "who is crazy?" The anxiety-induced answer is usually that it must be the person who uses the word psychoanalyst, psychiatrist, psychohistorian, psychologist, or psychotherapist.[2] Hi had a profound interest in the trauma caused by war and started "rap groups" for returning veterans to help them readjust to civilian life. His May 6, 1972 *New York Times* op-ed article, "Post-Vietnam Syndrome," helped educate vets and the public about one of the consequences of the war. When he heard that the category under which post-traumatic syndromes had been diagnosed was being eliminated from the *Diagnostic and Statistical Manual of Mental Disorders* (DSM), Shatan founded the Vietnam Veterans Working Group with colleagues, including Robert Jay Lifton. Under the new term, "Post-Traumatic Stress Disorder" (PTSD), which was developed in the Working Group, it was included in the DSM-III. He was a founding member of the Society for Traumatic Stress Studies, which later added the word "International" to its title.

As an organizer, I was initially delighted to have Chaim speak about and consider publishing on "bogus manhood." But I was soon disappointed when I realized that he wanted to give the same paper time after time, which he had been doing around the world at different professional conferences. Chaim frustrated me when he invariably and noisily came late to the small meetings of the Psychohistory Forum's communism and autobiography research groups. Although he could be annoying, I still miss Chaim, as I do so many others who befriended me in the building of psychohistory.

Shatan was but one of the many psychiatrists who made significant contributions to our field.[3] Sander Breiner (1925–2012), from the suburbs of Detroit, was a loyal IPA and Forum member who wrote on the history of childhood. William G. Niederland (1904–1993) was a zestful psychoanalytic psychiatrist who barely escaped the Holocaust and in the process of treating survivors helped develop the concept of survivor's guilt. He also made some early contributions to the field of psychogeography, a subject on which he presented at the Forum. When the IPA honored Niederland during a conference at Long Island University, individuals such as Peter Loewenberg and Vamık Volkan, who otherwise would never have come to the IPA in those days, attended. Jamshid Marvasti, an Iranian-American Connecticut psychiatrist, has a profound interest in the impact of war on those who serve in the U.S. military. He is a collaborative scholar who likes to work with younger colleagues, including those in the military. Alice Lombardo Maher is a Manhattan psychoanalyst and psychiatrist who after decades of private practice decided also to work with school children in her Changing Our Consciousness educational program to understand and mitigate conflicts among individuals and groups. She has brought in distinguished peacemakers, such as Vamık Volkan and Lord John Alderdice, who was knighted for helping resolve the conflict in Northern Ireland, to help young people understand conflict and establish dialogues to keep their enmities from leading to violent conflict. Mary Coleman is a retired physician who was passionately antiwar, often protesting outside of the White House. For many years, she inspired me to hold luncheon meetings of the Psychohistory Forum's War, Peace, and Conflict Resolution Research Group at the IPA. She eventually married the Israeli-American antiwar psychologist Jay Gonen, whose specialty is group psychohistory.[4] Jay came to America in graduate school and stayed not simply for a doctoral degree in psychology, but also because he had been sickened by the sight of many dead Egyptians during the Six-Day War. He made his career healing the psychic wounds of veterans in a Veterans Administration (VA) hospital in Chicago.

John Mack (1929–2004) is among the most famous of the psychoanalytic psychiatrists to make contributions to our field. His Pulitzer Prize-winning psychobiography, *A Prince of Our Disorder: The Life of T.E. Lawrence* (1976), was completed after twelve years of labor. Despite his many accomplishments, there was a strong movement to revoke his tenure at Harvard Medical School because in researching people claiming to have been abducted by aliens, he was seen as believing their stories and being unscientific. Fortunately, after a long, expensive, and very public struggle, his tenure was reaffirmed. He died when he was hit by a car crossing a dark London street while attending a conference. Regrettably, I never met him.[5]

Ralph Colp (1924–2008) was a tall, thin, ascetic Darwin scholar and a member of the Psychohistory Forum who made his living providing treatment to graduate students at Columbia University and through his private practice. Freud and Darwin were his lifelong ego ideals and studying Darwin was his passion. The ideal vacation of this shy man was to go to England, where he had befriended archivists to gather more information on the great naturalist. The great accomplishment of this erudite psychiatrist was to write about the medical history of Charles Darwin in *To Be An Invalid: The Illness of Charles Darwin* (1977). I proofed the greatly revised version, *Darwin's Illness* (2008), partly by his deathbed in the convalescence home on East 79th Street, half a block from his apartment where we had had so many stimulating Forum meetings. As I read my corrections and spoke, Ralph listened but did not speak. His youngest daughter, who flew in from her home in Israel, read to him as he awaited his death.[6]

I have two regrets regarding this dedicated psychohistorian. One, that I did not spend more time with him, since he wanted my company but was reluctant to ask directly. My sciatic leg and busy schedule did not allow me to drive to Manhattan as much as Ralph and I would have liked. The second is that I refused to take the offer that was transmitted through his wife that I take whatever books I wanted from his wonderful library on Darwin and Freud. I refused, because that seemed to be an acknowledgment of his impending death. In retrospect, I wish I had those mementos of Ralph, as I could have readily said, "I'm just borrowing them until you are better." After his death, his wife, who was also a medical doctor, sold his library. She had always quietly and ambivalently resented that Ralph devoted his time to Charles Darwin and psychohistory rather than to her and their two daughters. Acknowledgement of this was in the 1977 book dedication to his wife and daughters, who "lived with me, during the many years I lived with Charles Darwin."

Ken Fuchsman is an intellectual historian of the twentieth century whose very wide range of interests and knowledge includes Freud and the Oedipal complex. Ken told me he was doing psychohistory before he realized that there was an organized movement early in this century.[7] Together we teamed up to do psychobiographical studies, primarily of Barack Obama, over the course of which we had some very lively discussions, causing each of us to deepen our knowledge. I found him to be an excellent researcher, partly because he uses online sources so much more readily than I do. He became a very active member in the twenty-first century of the Forum and then the International Psychohistorical Association, of which he is now an activist president and bridge builder of psychohistory to academic historians and others. Fuchsman's major project is an ambitious book on the nature of being human.

Jacques Szaluta is a psychoanalytically trained European historian who wrote *Psychohistory: Theory and Practice* (1999), the only textbook of the field. Much of his scholarly focus has been on Freud's ego ideals, on which he has written a whole series of articles. Cinema has been a second area of considerable interest. He serves the Psychohistory Forum as moderator of its meetings, doing a wonderful job enabling me to be a much more active participant in the discussions. Jacques has also been a champion in defense of psychohistory among historians. Peter Webb Petschauer is another European-born historian who was drawn to psychohistory by his interest in childrearing and stayed because of his admiration for psychohistorians like Howard Stein and Vamık Volkan. I chronicled and analyzed at length the career of this fine colleague who had the misfortune of being born in 1939 in Berlin to a father who joined the SS diplomatic corps.[8] Despite his excellent contributions to psychohistory as a historian of childhood and women, as well as his evocative poetry, for decades Petschauer saw himself as an outsider to the psychohistorical movement, which I think relates to his having to live as an outsider throughout his childhood due to his family situation. He has shown a remarkable ability to thrive in the most diverse situations and empathize with varied individuals. In *The Face of Evil: The Sustenance of Tradition* (2014) Petschauer shows how four women who helped raise him survived under the Nazi regime. The election of President Trump troubled him so much that he said, "I was born under a fascist dictator and I don't intend to live under another one." Consequently, he and his American-born wife have been spending most of the year in Bavaria, where his daughter and only grandchild live.

There have been so many giving and wonderful colleagues who I have met in the course of doing psychohistory. Several individuals who stand out are Mary Lambert (1920–2012) and Lee and Connie Shneidman. Mary was a lovely lady whose family left Vienna to come to the United States when she was five. She was the epitome of elegance and grace. Mary was a social worker who trained as a psychoanalyst. She was in mourning for her musician/businessman husband who had recently died when she came to one of our Forum meetings in the late 1980s. She referred to it once as a "book club," resulting in my sharp comment about the very scholarly nature of what we did, and she never repeated what for me was a faux pas. She loved to host the Forum meetings in her wonderfully elegant Eastside apartment on the 32nd floor of 190 East 72nd Street in Manhattan. Colleagues appreciated her warm reception and were dazzled by the magnificent view of Central Park, the East River, and the city skyline. Their eyes would turn to the signed etchings by Miro, Signac, Marini, Sonja Delaunay, Renoir, Rouault; oils by Arthur Segal and Delle Site; and other art. I treasured Mary's friendship, insightful comments, and wise counsel. She insisted on serving coffee and pastries, despite my desire to end the practice of feeding the membership. I had given up after about twenty-five years of growing tired of bringing bagels and other goodies to the New York meetings. Hosting was becoming more and more difficult for her because of poor health, and after she stayed in her bedroom during a meeting once or twice with a home aide, I simply refused to accept her invitation to host. Subsequently, I visited Mary when I had meetings elsewhere in Manhattan.

Lee Shneidman (1929–2008) was a late medieval historian with a wide range of scholarly interests whose life had been shaped by hospitalizations following a life-threatening illness he suffered as a child. These experiences shaped his scholarship, since he wrote only of the Spanish empire's growth, never of decline. He had some analytic training, but in the first case had to stop because the Columbia Postgraduate Institute for Psychoanalytic Training would not allow a historian to progress to the point of seeing patients. Then, in Reuben Fine's institute, Lee left because he wanted to analyze deceased historical subjects and they wanted him to treat living patients. He believed communism to be an ideal system, but never Soviet communism, of which his father had been a supporter. Lee was a contrarian whose book on Jefferson's foreign policy was left unfinished at his death. I thought he had so much to say, to the point that I typed some of his handwritten essays on Marx and other subjects so I could publish them in *Clio's Psyche*. Connie (Connalee) Shneidman (1930–2007) was Lee's highly successful psychoanalyst and psychologist wife who, together with her husband, had written an early article on the Burr-Hamilton duel as Hamilton's suicide. At a Manhattan cocktail party, diminutive Connie met the six-foot eight-inch tall Paul Volcker, chair of the Federal Reserve, who asked what she did for a living. To her stating that she was a psychologist, he responded, "We're in the same business!" Clearly Volcker recognized the psychological aspects of economics, even if he never read one of *Clio's Psyche*'s articles on psychoeconomics. The Shneidmans were an erudite and delightful couple with a charming apartment on West 86th Street.[9]

When the Soviet Union collapsed in 1991, Lee, Ralph, Chaim, Mary, and others were so excited that I suggested the establishment of Communism: The Dream that Failed Research Group. My plan was to just start the group and then periodically check up on how it was doing, thus saving myself so many trips to New York. The Shneidmans, Ralph, and Mary had other ideas. They exuded such a warm desire to have my presence and the subject was so interesting that I continually drove into New York, muttering at times about how nice it would be to stay home and enjoy my wife's company and do more research on my own. I still can't drive past the 79th exit of the Henry Hudson Parkway without feeling some regret at the death of these fine colleagues. In 1999 we exhausted our interest in Marx and the decline of European communism, but the group was so reluctant to break up and miss the Shneidmans' lavish spread that it morphed into the Psychobiographical Autobiography Research Group. I kept driving to Manhattan.

Literary studies, beyond the psychobiographies of authors, were never a primary interest of mine, mostly because it was done so well elsewhere. Nevertheless, there were some wonderful literary scholars immersed in psychoanalysis I have had the pleasure of knowing and learning from. Andrew Brink (1932–2011) was an excellent scholar of Bertram Russell, the creativity of literary figures, and much more.[10] His ancestors settled the Hudson River Valley, which he left for Canada in protest over the United States' involvement in the Korean War. This thin, almost frail, man delighted in knowledge and apologized for not having had psychoanalysis as an adult. We became friends when, from my perspective of a scholar who was researching creativity connected to the early death of fathers, I reviewed one of his valuable books, which was focused on the creativity associated with early mother loss. We soon became friends seeing each other at the IPA and Forum meetings. In 1988, the leadership position of the Humanities and Psychoanalytic Thought Program at the University of Toronto became available. Andrew was very apologetic that despite his best efforts, he could not raise the funds to offer me the position, which unfortunately the University did not fund. Andrew had just retired from his professorship at McMaster University and being paid to further psychohistory was not important to him, so he assumed the Toronto position. He researched his Dutch pioneer ancestors, feeling quite guilty over their seventeenth-century war against Native Americans.[11] Dan Dervin is an emeritus professor of literature with a very broad psychohistorical focus, including creativity, film, literature, art, and the history of childhood.[12]

Independent scholars have made significant contributions to our field. Henry Lawton (1941–2014) was moved as a teenager by the fine psychohistorical book, *The Pursuit of the Millennium: Revolutionary Millenarians and Mystical Anarchists of the Middle Ages* (1957) by Norman Cohn (1915–2007). Cohn's book inspired Henry to try his own hand at psychohistory, resulting in his writing a master's dissertation on Richard Nixon. Although he made his living as a social worker, Henry aspired to be a scholar and an academic. After he became involved in organized psychohistory, he ultimately devoted every spare minute of his life to scholarship. Henry was extremely grateful to Lloyd deMause for accepting him on an equal basis with academics. He served the field as book review editor of *The Journal of Psychohistory*, secretary and later president of the IPA, and for a few years as co-director of the Psychohistory Forum, before he formed and directed the Group for the Psychohistorical Study of Film. *The Psychohistorian's Handbook* (1988) is flawed by its uncritical acceptance of some of deMause's poorly grounded theories, but it nevertheless has considerable value for the novice. His devotion to psychohistory was such that his family brought him in a wheelchair, despite enormous pain, to organize the registration table of the IPA's annual conference.

Melvin Kalfus (1931–2002) was an autodidact who loved history and made his living as a Madison Avenue advertising executive, where he rose to the position of senior vice president. As a scholar he is most remembered for his fine book, *Frederick Law Olmsted: The Passion of a Public Artist* (1990), but he had a wide range of interests and publications. He served the IPA as secretary, president, treasurer, and newsletter editor while earning a doctoral degree in history at NYU. Throughout his life, Kalfus suffered from ill health. At the dinner celebrating the award of his doctoral degree, I sat at a table with members of his cancer survivors group. In his final years he taught history as an adjunct professor of history in Florida, where I visited him in the winter.[13] Kalfus was good friends with Mel Goldstein (1926–1997), a Connecticut psychoanalyst, literature professor, and secular Jew, who looked like a Hasidic rabbi, greeted many of both sexes at the Psychohistory Forum and IPA with a bear hug, and for some years served as group process analyst at the IPA. Goldstein described his Sisyphean task of trying to teach medical students about feelings.[14]

The academic discipline of anthropology has been far more open to psychoanalysis than history or psychology, although few anthropologists have been affiliated with psychohistory. Among those few, Howard Stein stands out for his work. This gentle and brilliant man, who caused such an uproar with his early writings on Judaism, is the author of over thirty volumes on psychoanalytic, organizational, medical, and applied anthropology, including seven books of poetry.[15] From 1980 to 1989, he edited *The Journal of Psychoanalytic Anthropology* and was severely disappointed when the publisher decided to discontinue it for financial reasons. Upon graduating from Harvard, Eli Sagan (1927–2015) went into his family business instead of studying for a doctoral degree as a step toward a career in academia, but he never lost his love of knowledge.[16] He retired at age forty-seven so he could write books on subjects as varied as cannibalism and the reaction to modernity. Despite only having a bachelor's degree, his talents were recognized to the point where he was invited to teach without any prospect of earning tenure at great universities. Eli combined political action with his scholarship and was quite proud of having been twice listed on Nixon's Enemies List. Don Carveth is a charismatic Toronto-based psychoanalytic sociologist who, in his sixties, found a mentor in Sagan.[17] His own work is focused on the role of conscience.[18] Fawn Brodie (1915–1981) was an independent scholar who wrote such insightful psychoanalytic books on Thomas Jefferson, Nixon, Thaddeus Stevens, and the explorer Sir Richard Burton that she was accepted as a tenured professor in the UCLA history department despite her not having a doctoral degree.[19]

Many of the authors and scholars described above, the builders of psychohistory, have died. The "obligations of survival" is a term I use to explain why I have written and/or published a large number of memorials to contributors of psychohistory in the pages of *Clio's Psyche* and elsewhere. I feel that it is my duty while living to remember the dead. Clearly, there is some survivor's guilt involved. The murder in the Holocaust of most of my parents' families and the early death of brother, mother, and sister certainly have left their mark on me. Those who have done so much to build our field deserve to be remembered in all of their humanity.[20] So many deceased colleagues remain very much alive in my consciousness.

Holocaust survivors, their children, and those who have written about them appear to be quite open to a psychohistorical approach. Indeed, many of them have become psychoanalysts or other types of clinicians. Judith Kestenberg (1910–1999) was a dynamic little woman with whom I took my first psychoanalytic course, which was about childhood, and who created a major study on the impact of the Holocaust on Jewish children.[21] What she was not willing to share with others was that she barely escaped the Nazis. One psychoanalyst who worked on her project of documenting and deepening the understanding of the trauma of children under the Nazis remembered her being like an authoritarian parent who treated these accomplished colleagues as if they were children needing discipline. Another remembers her as brilliant, demanding, rigorous, and uncompromising.

Eva Fogelman is a talented psychoanalyst, filmmaker, and author who has immense gratitude for those who saved her father as he fled almost certain death in Nazi-occupied Eastern Europe. She wrote about the very small percentage of courageous people who were Christian rescuers. The most common characteristics of this diverse group was that they had had some sort of rescue experience in their own childhood and were raised in families who treated their children better relative to other families in that time. Eva integrated psychohistorical concepts on childrearing directly into her book and is currently working on a book about women in the Holocaust.[22] Flora Hogman is a New York psychologist whose sense of identity was severely damaged by the fact that she was a hidden child in Vichy, France and lost both her parents. As a young adult, she rediscovered her lost Jewish identity and made a career as a psychologist. Hogman hosted Forum meetings for years and shared her life with my students. Isaac Zieman (1920–2007) was an extraordinarily courageous reconciler of Germans, Christians, Muslims, and Jews. His entire family was killed by their Latvian neighbors when the Nazis arrived, and he survived in Stalin's gulag. Isaac was so driven to make the world a better place that he left his hospital bed to deliver his talk on reconciliation of former enemies to the Forum shortly before his death. Except for some of the hidden children, those who came to psychohistory as Holocaust survivors, like Zieman, have mostly died.

William "Bill" J. Gilmore (1945–1999) aided psychohistory in two important ways. He hosted the 1976 Stockton State conference and, far more significantly, he wrote *Psychohistorical Inquiry: A Comprehensive Research Bibliography* (1984). Several times he came to the Institute for Psychohistory to do a type of opposition research for his friends in GUPH and the *Psychohistory Review*. Clearly, Bill Gilmore hated deMause.

Bruce Mazlish (1923–2016) took great pride in being an early historian member of Wellfleet and advocate of psychohistory. He edited *Psychoanalysis and History* (1963, 1971), taught psychohistory into the 1980s, and wrote some psychobiographical studies.[23] Regrettably, when academia mostly turned against psychohistory he stopped working in the area, instead devoting himself to global history and creating a film series especially useful for those who taught World Civilization courses.[24]

For reasons of his own personality, Lloyd deMause often worked through surrogates, some of whom, like Henry Ebel and Casper Schmidt, were both quite brilliant and outrageous at times. Their often wild ideas somehow empowered him to push his psychohistorical speculations to the extreme, usually without any real evidence. I can remember being thrilled by deMause's identification with newborn babies as he reported on the work of Leboyer, who empathized with newborn babies being born in sterile hospitals and spanked on their behinds. However, someone like Casper Schmidt could encourage Lloyd to take his notions of the importance of fetal life to degrees far beyond the scientific evidence of the period, and perhaps any period. Glenn Davis was bright and even less stable than Ebel and Schmidt, but not nearly as creative. However, deMause found him to be a useful vehicle to express his ideas about childhood in America. Glenn wrote *Childhood and History in America* (1977) before committing suicide by jumping off the George Washington Bridge after his doctoral dissertation was rejected at CUNY. Jerrold Atlas is not known for creativity, but rather for his chutzpah; over the years, several of our colleagues have wondered about his claim to have made numerous contributions to psychohistory. True, he brought considerable energy to it, including running mid-year conferences at Long Island University, well before being detenured there. But his claim to run a psychohistorical university on the Internet seems to have no merit; an extensive search there has not revealed its existence.

Molly Castelloe deserves credit for establishing an online message board (listserv) for *Clio's Psyche*.[25] She has also proven herself to be a fine filmmaker with *Vamık's Room* (2016), popularizing the peacemaking work of Vamık Volkan. Inna Rozentsvit recently came to psychohistory, bringing enormous dedication and energy. She is a powerful bridge to the psychoanalytic community, who researches and writes extensively as well as filming meetings to leave an online record.[26]

Popularizers of psychoanalysis often became strong advocates of psychohistory. Lucy Freeman (1917–2005) was a pioneer female *New York Times* reporter and author of over seventy books who played an important role as a popularizer of psychoanalysis and mental health issues, heralding their benefits to a very large number of Americans. In her later years, she hosted a Forum meeting in her apartment overlooking Central Park. Flora Rheta Schreiber (1918–1988) was a New York English professor, journalist, and the author of the 1973 bestseller *Sybil*, about a woman who allegedly had sixteen different personalities. In 1983, she published *The Shoemaker*, documenting the story of serial killer Joseph Kallinger, who was diagnosed with paranoid schizophrenia. Flora was theatrical in her presentation, and I came to doubt her scholarship and judgment. For example, she had one of Kallinger's sons, who had participated in his father's murders, move into her Gramercy Park apartment where she had hosted Forum meetings.

Bob Lentz is an extraordinarily capable American living in Canada. We met at the 1994 IPA meeting, and I selected him as associate editor when I started *Clio's Psyche* as a newsletter in 1994. There was a Rutgers professor who was experienced as a newsletter editor and was quite willing to work with me on this project, but I just had the feeling that Bob Lentz is an excellent person, despite his having no advanced degrees and no real background in psychohistory. He was a terrific choice. For nine years, Bob served as associate editor, doing virtually all our work at a distance except for the week that he visited me, teaching me about the new, more powerful computer system, which some unknown person donated to the Forum. Bob, who had the confidential instincts of a CIA agent, insisted he was not the donor. This new computer meant that we could communicate electronically between his home in Canada and my home office in New Jersey. Lentz was a real workhorse who demonstrated excellent judgment. He often helped to keep me grounded. For those first nine years of rapid growth, he deserves enormous credit. Upon his retirement as associate editor, no one replaced him because he is indeed irreplaceable. Bob continued to serve as an editor, confidant, and a most trusted member of our confidential referees for the next fifteen years. I cannot say enough in praise of this extraordinarily competent human being who refused to write for *Clio*, except occasionally as an interviewer of featured scholars.

C. Fred Alford is a talented and prolific scholar who has the well-deserved position of Distinguished Scholar-Teacher at the University of Maryland.[27] As a psychoanalytically grounded political scientist, he writes about moral psychology and much else. Fred's devotion to furthering the psychodynamic paradigm applied to contemporary and historical society also takes the form of supporting the Association for the Psychoanalysis of Culture and Society (APCS) and the Forum.

Charles B. Strozier, who was one of the key members of GUPH, editor of the *Psychohistory Review*, and one of very few professors to have an appointment in psychohistory, at first insisted that one could not function properly as a historian and simultaneously as a psychoanalyst. This opinion was formed in part by the

Chicago Training Institute he attended, allowing historians to attend classes but not see patients without a waiver to become a psychoanalyst. When living in the Midwest, he declared on a number of occasions that becoming a psychoanalyst would interfere with being a proper historian. After Strozier moved to New York, he rapidly continued his psychoanalytic training, began to practice analysis, and became very active in the psychoanalytic community. I wondered if his early hesitancy about practicing as a psychoanalyst was related to the Chicago Institute's policies. He has had a very productive career as co-director of Robert Lifton's Center on Violence and Human Survival, director of the John Jay Center on Terrorism, a Lincoln scholar, and a prolific author on the dangers of apocalypticism.[28]

As a psychohistorian, I have a good deal of empathy for academic psychologists devoted to writing psychobiography and teaching in psychology departments.[29] The study of lives in their entirety is disdained by the psychologists dominating university psychology departments.[30] These psychologists encourage personality research, searching for variables and usually losing sight of the whole person in the process. William McKinley Runyan, as a graduate student at Harvard, was not only told that studying life histories was unscientific, but it was suggested that he leave graduate school by a leader of his field. Fortunately, "Mac" Runyan persevered, encouraged by retired professors Henry Murray[31] and Robert White, who came from an earlier psychological tradition, and went on to write *Life Histories and Psychobiographies: Explorations in Theory and Method* (1982) and additional publications on psychohistory and psychobiography.

His like-minded friend, Alan Elms, took his psychology doctoral degree at Yale, wrote about whole people, and taught at Davis in the University of California system, whose psychology departments were perhaps less hostile to scholars with his interests than most throughout the nation. They are part of a movement within academic psychology to build the field of personality psychology, which includes personology (the study of lives). The Society for Personology has provided valuable support for others, including James W. Anderson, editor of the *Annual of Psychoanalysis* and a member of the Editorial Board of *Clio's Psyche*, as they practice their craft. These mavericks within academic psychology have a clear presence in California and some are members of the East Bay Psychobiography Group, which is not mostly comprised of academics. One of the younger members of this group is William Todd Schultz, who put together a valuable selection of articles in *The Handbook of Psychobiography* (2005). Regrettably, in this volume Schultz ignores the psychobiography being written by historians, members of the IPA and the Psychohistory Forum, and most others, which is why I labeled my positive review "Separate Psychobiographical Tents, Separate Struggles."[32]

I am less qualified to assess the psychohistory of academic psychologists than of historians, political scientists, and psychoanalysts.[33] Anderson, who is well qualified, sees the work of his colleagues as a significant area of psychohistory. They created the Society for Qualitative Inquiry in Psychology as a subdivision of the American Psychological Association and produce *Qualitative Psychology*, which

sometimes publishes psychobiographical articles.[34] There is also an online newsletter for which Anderson writes a column. Joseph Ponterotto, an academic psychologist and psychobiographer of Bobby Fischer and John F. Kennedy, Jr., is
an advocate in the same movement who has published valuable articles on psychobiography in psychology and psychobiographical training for psychologists.[35]
That these were published in African and European psychology journals may be
an indication of a lack of receptivity in North America. Burton Norman Seitler,
a psychoanalyst member of the Psychohistory Forum, in 2017 started *JASPER
INTERNATIONAL: Journal for the Advancement of Scientific Psychoanalytic Empirical
Research*, which I see as rather psychohistorical.

My association with Lloyd deMause and the IPA meant that there were some
very fine psychohistorians who would have little or nothing to do with me for
many years because of their strong feelings about the damage they felt Lloyd had
done to our field. I met John Putnam Demos at a Rutgers University conference at which he was presenting with Peter Loewenberg. I was impressed with
the fine work that this Yale early American historian was doing, work that had
won him a Bancroft Prize and other awards.[36] It became clear to both Peter and
John that I was very much my own man and so their resistance to associate with
me was clearly lessened. Incidentally, if anyone confused John's similar surname
with deMause he all but exploded! John came and spoke to the History Club
at Ramapo College and I got to know him somewhat. It is interesting that this
author of two books on witchcraft discovered that he was related to a participant
in the Salem witch trials. Thomas Kohut, the historian son of the famous psychoanalyst Heinz Kohut, trained as a psychoanalyst in Cincinnati and became a
professor of history at Williams College. Tom and I corresponded and he made it
clear that I was too close to deMause and the IPA for him to become involved
with *Clio's Psyche*. However, he accepted writing about dual training in history
and psychoanalysis and becoming a featured scholar in *Clio's Psyche* when these
ideas were endorsed by Peter Loewenberg; he also co-authored an obituary for
Robert Waite, who was a colleague of his at Williams.

Lawrence J. Friedman, an extraordinarily accomplished psychobiographer of
the Menningers, Erikson, and Fromm, corresponded with me over the years and
eventually joined the Forum, where he gave some very impressive presentations
after his retirement from Indiana University and assumption of a position at Harvard. Larry is one of those out of area members of the Forum who only makes
the long trip to meetings when he has something to present, which has always
been welcomed. Friedman was an active member of the Wellfleet group, whose
longevity and accomplishments I greatly admire.[37]

David Lotto is a longtime Forum member who has an impressive ability to
work with disparate groups. He was able to join the Wellfleet Group rather late in
his existence when he offered a paper to Lifton on vengeance. He simultaneously
stayed so close to Lloyd deMause that he was accepted as co-editor and then editor of *The Journal of Psychohistory* once Lloyd's memory problems prevented him

from maintaining this labor of love. David restored the refereeing system that David Beisel had maintained when he was editor of the *Journal* from 1980–1989. He is a quiet man whose strong antiwar feelings led him to move to Canada during the Vietnam War. Sometimes, to my mind, there is a tension between his left-wing politics and his approach as a psychohistorian. I have always found him to be a cooperative colleague and I appreciate the work he's doing for the *Journal*.

Psychohistory may be centered in the U.S., but it is in fact a worldwide movement. Europeans fleeing Hitler did so much to develop psychohistory in the U.S., but what of postwar psychohistory in Europe? Many Europeans have written fine psychohistory. Alexander Mitscherlich, the author of *The Inability to Mourn: Principles of Collective Behaviour* (with his wife, Margarete; the original German work was published in 1967) and *Society Without the Father: A Contribution to Social Psychology* (the original German work was published in 1963), focused on Germans' reactions, and lack thereof, to the war, the Holocaust, and the loss of their leader. As an organized movement, psychohistory came to Germany primarily as a result of Germans who attended conferences in the U.S. and/or published in *The Journal of Psychohistory*, mostly as a result of David Beisel and Lloyd deMause reaching out to them.[38] As I seek to remember the names of these colleagues, some who come to mind are Gerhard Bliersbach, Christian Büttner, Aurel Ende, Ralph Frenken, Ludwig Janus, Rudolf Kreis, Winfried Kurth, Christian Lackner, Peter Orban, Gert Raeithel, Heinrich J. Reiss, and Helm Stierlin. In Germany, ten volumes of *Jahrbuch der Kindheit* (Translation: *Yearbook of Childhood*) were published (1984–1993), and since 2000 the annual *Jahrbuch für psychohistorische Forschung* (Translation: *Yearbook for Psychological Research*) has been regularly published.[39]

Jacques Szaluta reports that his *La psychohistoire* was published in France in 1987.[40] The first printing was of sixteen thousand copies and he reports he came across it being displayed in the book section of a Paris department store. Rudolph Binion had worked in Paris for six years in the late 1940s and early 1950s and published the booklet *Introduction à la psychohistoire* in 1982. A French psychohistory group and the journal, *Or le temps: Revue Française de Psychohistoire* (1994–2000), were created, but the field never took hold to the extent it has in Germany. Certainly, there are a few colleagues like Robert-Louis Liris and Marc-André Cotton who have done or are doing psychohistorical work.

For many years multi-talented American-born Brett Kahr ran psychohistory meetings in London, but finally gave up due to a lack of interest. Paul Ziolo lists himself as a psychohistorian at the University of Liverpool. Recently, Nick Duffell, who categorizes himself as a psychotherapist and psychohistorian, mentioned that he was considering starting a psychohistory group with a colleague. Fortunately, psychoanalysis has taken hold in the U.K., and numbers of Brits are associated with the Association for the Psychoanalysis of Culture and Society and its journal. Under the banner of psychosocial studies, colleagues there appear to be doing a good deal of activities that I would call psychohistory.

Elsewhere, Stefan Borbély translated some of David Beisel's and my psychohistory into Romanian. Alenka Puhar from Slovenia was actively discussing Balkan swaddling and other aspects of childrearing. Tomasz Pawelec and a few other young Polish historians expressed an interest in psychohistory in the 1990s, but they did not become committed to the field. In Hungary, there is Zsuzsanna Agora. Some young historians in Belarus, such as Dmitry Samakhvalau, became interested in psychohistory and had some conferences in Minsk. Olga Shutova came from Minsk to the U.S. as a young professor with a doctoral degree when David Beisel asked me to chaperone her on one occasion because some colleagues seemed more interested in her beauty than her quest for knowledge.[41] According to Juhani Ihanus, in 1997 in Minsk, Olga published the first Russian language psychohistory book, *Психоистория: школа и методы* (Translation: *Psychohistory: Schools and Methods*). Life in a dictatorship is not conducive to psychohistory and Olga now lives in Paris. Inna Rozentsvit, a psychoanalyst and Psychohistory Forum Research Associate who is an energetic advocate for psychoanalysis, is working to bring psychohistory to the Russian-speaking world.

Finland has been more fertile ground for psychohistory, with Juhani Ihanus and Juha Siltala making contributions. In 2001, Ihanus published in English *Swaddling, Shame and Society: On Psychohistory and Russia*. In Switzerland, there are a couple of psychohistorians, including the economist Florian Galler. In Austria, Artur R. Boelderl has been active in psychohistory. In 1997, one of my articles on Bob Dole was republished in Spain in *psicología política*. As editor of *Clio's Psyche* I have published at least one psychohistorical article by a Portuguese colleague.

Postwar European psychohistory is mostly an offshoot of American psychohistory, just as U.S. psychohistory developed from Viennese roots. In most areas of Europe, it remains fairly rudimentary and there is a marked deMausian influence.

A deficit of this study is that it fails to sufficiently cover our colleagues around the world; that is for others to do. I wish to apologize to the numerous colleagues who have done so much for our field who are not mentioned here. I know that there are many who quietly do their work without encountering me. I especially would like to know more about these talented colleagues in California's Psychoanalytic Consortium and in Chicago, South America, and Australia. In addition, there are other centers of psychohistory that I simply haven't had the pleasure of knowing about, or knowing well enough, to include here, given the limits of time and space. Perhaps they will write their own articles, chapters, and books about their experiences in psychohistory. I certainly would be eager to read these.

Notes

1 Some colleagues whose scholarly lives have been devoted totally to psychohistory are David Beisel, Lloyd deMause, Melvin Kalfus, Henry Lawton, Robert Jay Lifton, Peter Loewenberg, Elizabeth Marvick, Jacques Szaluta, and me.

2 Because the language of psychology has permeated our society so much more than forty years ago when Shatan first made this point to me, it is less the case now than it was then.

3 In the psychohistorical movement, there are no tests for doctrinal purity. For example, Peter Barglow is a West Coast psychiatrist who maintains a membership in the Psychohistory Forum and writes an occasional paper for *Clio's Psyche* while admiring

and agreeing with Fred Crews, the arch anti-Freudian. Yet in comprehending complex historical figures and some sick patients, he sometimes finds the language of psychoanalysis to be meaningful and a help.

4 Paul H. Elovitz, "An Intellectual Partnership: Jay Gonen and Mary Coleman," *Clio's Psyche*, Vol. 7 No. 4 (March 2001): pp. 167, 189–198. Two of Jay's books are *A Psychohistory of Zionism* (1975) and *The Roots of Nazi Psychology: Hitler's Utopian Barbarism* (2000).

5 Paul H. Elovitz, "John Mack (1929–2004): In Memoriam," *Clio's Psyche*, Vol. 12 No. 2 (September 2005): pp. 108–110.

6 Paul H. Elovitz, "Ralph Colp: Darwin Scholar and Psychiatrist," *Clio's Psyche*, Vol. 15 No. 3 (December 2008): pp. 105, 160–162.

7 Paul H. Elovitz, "Ken Fuchsman: Scholar of the Human Condition," *Clio's Psyche*, Vol. 23 No. 3 (Spring 2017): pp. 310–325.

8 Paul H. Elovitz, "The Impact of a Psychohistorian's Life Experience and Personality on His Career and Scholarship," *The Journal of Psychohistory*, Vol. 42 (Summer 2015): pp. 53–70.

9 Paul H. Elovitz, "J. Lee Shneidman: Historian," *Clio's Psyche*, Vol. 10 No. 1 (June 2003): pp. 26–31; Paul H. Elovitz, "In Memoriam: Connalee Shneidman," *Clio's Psyche*, Vol. 13 No. 4 (March 2007): pp. 224–226.

10 Paul H. Elovitz, "The Creativity of Andrew Brink" (Featured Scholar Interview), *Clio's Psyche*, Vol. 6 No. 2 (September 1999): pp. 76–82.

11 Andrew Brink, *Invading Paradise: Esopus Settlers at War with Natives, 1659, 1663* (2003).

12 Dervin is the author of at least eight books, including *Bernard Shaw: A Psychological Study* (1975); *A Strange Sapience: Psychoanalytic Study of Creativity in D. H. Lawrence* (1984); *Through a Freudian Lens Deeply: A Psychoanalysis of the Cinema* (1985); *Creativity and Culture* (1990*); Enactments: American Modes and Psychohistorical Models* (1996); *Matricentric Narratives: Recent British Women's Fiction in a Postmodern Mode* (1997); and *Home Is Another Country* (1998). He has a book on childhood in press.

13 Paul H. Elovitz, et al., "In Memoriam: Melvin Kalfus (1931–2002)," *Clio's Psyche*, Vol. 9 No. 1 (June 2002): pp. 48–53.

14 Paul H. Elovitz, "In Memoriam: Melvin Goldstein (1926–1997)," *Clio's Psyche*, Vol. 4 No. 1 (June 1997): pp. 32–33.

15 Howard Stein's numerous publications include *Listening Deeply: An Approach to Understanding and Consulting in Organizational Culture* (1994); *The Dream of Culture* (1994); *The Human Cost of a Management Failure: Organizational Downsizing at General Hospital* (1996-co-authored), and *Developmental Time, Cultural Space: Studies in Psychogeography* (2013).

16 Paul H. Elovitz, "Eli Sagan: Scholar of Aggression and Sociologist," *Clio's Psyche*, Vol. 8, No. 1 (June 2001): pp. 31–39.
    Sagan's books include *Cannibalism: Human Aggression and Cultural Form* (1974); *The Lust to Annihilate: A Psychoanalytic Study of Violence in Ancient Greek Society* (1979); *At the Dawn of Tyranny: The Origins of Individualism, Political Oppression, and the State* (1985); *Freud, Women, and Morality: The Psychology of Good and Evil* (1988); *The Honey and The Hemlock: Democracy and Paranoia in Ancient Athens and Modern America* (1991); and *Citizens and Cannibals: The French Revolution, the Struggle for Modernity, and the Origins of Ideological Terror* (2001).

17 Donald Carveth, "My Mentor Eli Sagan (1927–2015): In Memoriam," *Clio's Psyche*, Vol. 22 Nos.1–2 (June–September 2015): pp. 110–115.

18 Paul H. Elovitz, "Don Carveth: Psychoanalytic Sociologist," *Clio's Psyche*, Vol. 13 No.1 (June 2006): pp. 66–74.

19 The "Fawn M. Brodie 25 Year Retrospective" had articles by eleven authors (*Clio's Psyche*, Vol. 13 No. 1 (June 2006): pp. 1, 29–66).

20 Interviewing and publishing the work of so many distinguished colleagues is time consuming, yet quite gratifying. Writing memorials is painful and I am often heard to say that any issue of *Clio* without a memorial is an especially good issue.

21 Among her many books are Judith Kestenberg and Charlotte Kahn, *Children Surviving Persecution: An International Study of Trauma and Healing* (Westport, CT: Praeger, 1998) and with Ira Brenner, *The Last Witness: The Child Survivor of the Holocaust* (1996).

22 Eva Fogelman, *Conscience and Courage: Rescuers of Jews in the Holocaust* (1995).

23 His books included *James and John Stuart Mill: Father and Son in the Nineteenth Century* (New York: Basic Books, 1972) and *The Revolutionary Ascetic: Evolution of a Political Type* (New York: Basic Books, 1976).

24 Paul H. Elovitz, "Bruce Mazlish (1923–2016): In Memoriam," *Clio's Psyche*, Vol. 23 No. 3 (Spring 2017): pp. 326–328.

25 In the 1990s Michael Hirohama of California had also established a listserv for the Psychohistory Forum and *Clio's Psyche*. Both Hirohama and Castelloe received Sidney Halpern (monetary) Awards for their efforts.

26 Some of these meeting recordings may be found at cliospsyche.org and others may be found on the IPA website.

27 Paul H. Elovitz, "C. Fred Alford: Professor of Government and Distinguished Scholar-Teacher," *Clio's Psyche*, Vol. 13 No. 4 (March 2007): pp. 179, 204–210.

28 Paul H. Elovitz, "A Conversation with Charles B. Strozier," *Clio's Psyche*, Vol. 3 No. 4 (March 1997): pp. 97, 120–126.

29 Academic psychologists like John Hartman, who taught in the psychiatry department of the University of Michigan, did not have these problems.

30 Joseph Ponterotto of Fordham University argues that this is more of a "past" attitude and that there is a renaissance in psychobiography, quoting Zoltan Kovary's review, 2011, in *Europe's Journal of Psychology*, as reflected in the *American Psychologist*, July/August 2017 issue, which devoted a whole special section to psychobiography.

31 See James W. Anderson, "An Interview with Henry A. Murray on His Meeting with Sigmund Freud," *Psychoanalytic Psychology*, Vol. 34 (2017): pp. 322–331.

32 *The Journal of Psychohistory*, Vol. 34 No. 1 (Summer 2006): pp. 83–93.

33 In the 1970s I started attending the meetings of the New Jersey Psychoanalytic Society with great enthusiasm; however, I soon lost interest since I was looking for psychobiography and psychohistory, of which I found almost none. There were some interesting case studies presented by the psychiatrists and some papers on Freud and other psychoanalysts, but I saw no inclination to break new ground. In discussing Freud, there was sometimes a quality of Biblical exegesis. As psychoanalytically-inspired scholars we build on Freud's brilliant work, but we must also go beyond what he accomplished.

34 Harold Takooshian, a Fordham University psychologist who has hosted Psychohistory Forum meetings for two years, sent me the impressive program of the Society for the Qualitative Inquiry in Psychology 2017 program of its two-day meetings with numerous presentations. Regrettably, from the titles of the papers delivered I found no evidence of psychobiography or psychohistory.

35 Joseph G. Ponterotto, "Psychobiography in Psychology: Past, Present, and Future," *Journal of Psychology in Africa*, Vol. 25 No. 5 (2015): pp. 379–389 and Joseph G. Ponterotto, Jason D Reynolds, Samantha Morel, and Linda Cheung, "Psychobiographical Training in Psychology in North America: Mapping the Field and Charting a Course," *Europe's Journal of Psychology*, Vol. 11 No. 3 (2015): pp. 459–475.

36 Some of Demos' noteworthy books include *Entertaining Satan: Witchcraft and the Culture of Early New England* (1982); *A Little Commonwealth: Family Life in Plymouth Colony*

(1999); *The Unredeemed Captive: A Family Story from Early America* (1995); and *The Enemy Within: 2,000 Years of Witch-Hunting in the Western World* (2008).

37 Because of issues of age and declining health, Robert Jay Lifton had the last yearly Wellfleet meetings in 2015, although group members continued to meet in New York for a yearly lunch.

38 When he was editor of *The Journal of Psychohistory* for nine years, Beisel not only solicited articles from various Europeans, but also arranged for Gerhard Bliersbach, Aurel Ende, Gert Raeithel, and Alenka Puhar to become Contributing Editors of the *Journal*.

39 I am indebted to Peter Petschauer and especially Juhani Ihanus for help with these materials on European psychohistory.

40 In English, *Psychohistory: Theory and Practice* (1999).

41 Professor Shutova wrote to Lloyd deMause asking where she could best learn psychohistory in the U.S. on a year-long sabbatical for that purpose. He said she should come and take David Beisel's psychohistory courses at Rockland Community College of the State University of New York, which she did. She also attended Saturday meetings of the Psychohistory Forum. Beisel's talents as a professor, especially of psychohistory, were such that many of his colleagues audited his courses and many adult students attended them as well. Beisel's career was shaped by the de-tenuring of faculty at Pace University where he first taught, the poor job market in history, and prejudices against psychohistory. Otherwise, a man of his talents would have taught at a major university. As it was he won various awards for his teaching, and his scholarship is first rate. See Peter Petschauer and Paul H. Elovitz, "David Beisel: Psychohistorian Extraordinaire," *Psychohistory News*, Vol. 36 No. 3 (Summer 2017): pp. 5–7.

14

CONCLUDING THOUGHTS

My half century doing psychohistory has been a wonderful, enlightening, and at times frustrating journey. It has been enlightening and wonderful because of the camaraderie I experienced with colleagues, the psychological tools I learned, and the opportunity to apply these insights to the world, history, and myself. It has also been frustrating because of the intense resistance in academia, divisions among psychohistorians, and leadership missteps. Opponents of psychological history have sometimes deluded themselves into thinking that psychohistory was just a passing fancy that is now dead and gone. My focus has overwhelmingly been on the positive, including the colleagues I encountered as a psychohistorical editor and leader.

Why people come to the organized field of psychohistory has long interested me. As an Eriksonian participant-observer, I start with myself to find the answer. I was excited by the deeper view of history that was provided when the irrational and the unconscious were brought into it, since they had not been a part of my graduate training. Unbeknownst to me at the time, I was searching for tools to better understand myself, my relationships with others, and the problems in my marriage. As an organizer of psychohistory for over four decades, I have also observed why others come to my field.

Most are drawn to the field by the possibility of gaining new and deeper insights into the human condition. Those who are psychoanalysts or greatly influenced by depth psychology find it easy to accept meaningful interpretations of people individually and in groups. When psychologically inclined individuals became concerned by what is happening in the public arena, they start looking for the knowledge we possess. Thus when Richard Nixon was showing signs of self-defeating behavior in front of the nation, a market developed for psychobiographies of our thirty-seventh president. In subsequent elections there have been psychological studies of the major candidates. Authors of biographies often turn to our knowledge for a deeper understanding of their subjects. Some come to psychohistory in lieu of analysis, often as in my case, because they didn't even consciously know they needed it. Those who see the field as a purely intellectual activity and haven't undergone meaningful therapy will never really understand much about the unconscious.[1] Ideally, to do the best possible work, a psychohistorian should be psychoanalyzed, but in fact some, like Peter Petschauer and Henry Lawton before he entered analysis, have done invaluable work without it.

Psychoanalytic and psychohistorical ideas spread not primarily through the conferences and journals specifically devoted to them, but through books, television, and articles that adopt and disseminate them. A certain level of motivational insight simply becomes part of the culture. Prior to Freud and psychohistory, this psychological insight just wasn't present. Since psychohistory has been shunned by the academic psychology and history departments, a common, conscious or unconscious solution is to kill the messenger while taking the message. For example, in Ian Kershaw's almost 900-page *Hitler 1889–1936: Hubris* (2000), psychobiography, psychohistory, psychology, and psychoanalysis don't appear in the index, as pointed out by David Beisel.[2] The author specifically rejects psychological analysis, but his interpretation nevertheless has numerous psychological explanations.[3]

"What happened to you guys? I thought psychohistory was going to be the next big thing?" This question was put to me in 2006 by the late Peter Novick (1934–2012), Professor of History at the University of Chicago and winner of the American Historical Association's 1989 prize for the best book of the year in American history, *That Noble Dream: The "Objectivity Question" and the American Historical Profession*. I responded that we mostly do good work in the face of stiff academic resistance, but we may have to wait for a new generation of scholars to be accepted in the halls of ivy. In contrast to most of the historical profession, Novick was appreciative of psychoanalytically based insights, having dedicated one of his books to his analyst.

Political opinions also play a role in some scholars' journey to psychohistory. There's always been a left of center inclination among significant numbers of the International Psychohistorical Association. Many see psychohistory as an instrument for social change. Of course, this goes beyond the IPA, since most members of the Wellfleet Group shared the same tendency, as does Lifton. I think of one of the loyal members of the Forum and a valuable contributor to *Clio's Psyche*. For many years I had to ask this member, who shall remain anonymous, to revise his articles, urging him to write as a psychoanalyst and psychohistorian rather than as a political radical. Most who had been Marxist gave up this belief well before coming to our field; however, a few held to their anti-capitalist ideals of an earlier period. As editor, I tried to be equally accepting of colleagues regardless of their political orientation, although the anonymous referees don't necessarily agree.

Antiwar feelings have always tended to be strong among my colleagues, as reflected in the large turnout I got for luncheon IPA sessions on war, peace, and conflict resolution. Both Lifton and deMause have always had strong antiwar leanings. Several important contributors had moved to Canada to avoid the Korean and Vietnam drafts. In the 1990s, the IPA received a gift of stock worth about three thousand dollars from Roger Lorenz, who lived in Washington State in a mountainside cabin without electricity or running water, precisely because he thought Lloyd deMause's ideas could lead to a world without war. In World War II, Roger had refused to serve because he decided that it was wrong to kill. He subsequently refused to pay federal taxes because some of the money was used for war or possible war. When he inherited some stock, he gave half to the IPA and the other half to another nonprofit organization so he would not have to pay taxes on this money.[4]

The personal and professional journey that I have described in these pages opened enormous opportunities to me, even if it did not further my academic career. Perhaps the latter part of this statement isn't accurate, since when I tried to write prior to discovering psychohistory I overwhelmingly encountered writer's block, even while starting a book of English Industrial Revolution documents for which a German publisher had given me a small advance. Once I began writing as a psychohistorian, the writer's block diminished and then disappeared. I can now proudly say that I have over three hundred and fifty publications. At Ramapo College, which I continue to love and proudly serve, psychohistory cost me when it came to personnel decisions. My failure to be promoted to full professor, despite my hundreds of publications and receipt of the Ramapo Alumni Association Faculty Award for Leadership, Teaching, and Dedication (1990) and other awards was based on prejudice against psychohistory and not being a master of academic politics. I was told that one of the arguments used against my last application for promotion was that there were only four American Historical Association members who listed psychohistory as their field. This argument was made in a college that prides itself on being interdisciplinary—at least in theory![5] As is the case with almost all psychological historians, decades ago I gave up my membership in the AHA because of the prejudice of the leadership against psychohistory.

In this volume I have shared a full sense of my exuberant journey, especially in the early years of organized psychohistory, as well as my response to the academic resistance that is inclined to be strongest in psychology and history departments. I am proud of the staying power that I have had, which unfortunately is not characteristic of so many others drawn to psychohistory. There are strong personal roots to this endurance. I suspect this ability is related to my being the youngest of three children and feeling that while I was not necessarily the favored one, I would be the most loyal.[6] Tragically, death took my sister and brother, whose pictures I look at with both great affection and sadness. I remained as the surviving child with all the benefits and responsibilities that followed when my father was in decline prior to his death of a broken heart. His will to live was destroyed by a world that had taken his beloved wife, two of his three children, and then a grandchild by a disease, HIV/AIDS, that was so horrible that no one in the family dared say its name. My staying power is such that as of the end of the Spring 2018 semester, I will be the only remaining founding faculty member at Ramapo College. So it is not just in psychohistory that I have expressed this inclination to stick it out in good times and bad. I have never liked separations and have sometimes joked that I started the Saturday workshop of the Institute for Psychohistory so as to avoid a long separation from colleagues who were doing such important and exciting work.

My mother raised me to be a secular *Yeshiva Bucher*—that is, a student of the Talmud. Incidentally, her father, before he changed his religion from Judaism to socialism in Tsarist Russia, had a position in the synagogue, which was an honor among Eastern European Jews. I often joke that I am addicted to school—a school-a-holic. My field of study became not the Hebraic Bible and the Talmud, but rather a modern equivalent created by the atheist Freud and his followers. Reading, working with, and learning from psychohistorical colleagues such as Binion, deMause, Gay, Lifton, Loewenberg, and Volkan greatly enlarged my understanding of the human condition. It has been a pleasure to share this knowledge with my students and colleagues throughout the years. Because I opted to teach at a small college they have, with one exception,[7] always been undergraduate students. Psychoanalysis, with its emphasis on the individual experience, saved me from falling into the burnout that so often afflicts professors; this is because I continue to see my students as separate individuals rather than slow learners, as is so commonly the case among professors.

Rather than teach graduate students, which is the aim of most young PhDs, I have had the challenge and pleasure of teaching in the postgraduate setting I established in the Saturday workshops of the Institute for Psychohistory and then the Psychohistory Forum. When there was greater interest in psychohistory, I used to have a brochure listing a dozen presentations over a two-year period, including the subjects, pictures of the presenters, and brief biographies. As the ranks of academia closed against our field, fewer colleagues have come forth with proposals. In fact, some colleagues and I have become the presenters much more frequently than in the earlier years. My becoming a presidential psychobiographer and psychohistorian, which I can partly credit to Lloyd deMause, has been a monumental challenge because of the complexities involved in America's permanent presidential campaign.

Finding my own voice in relationship to colleagues like Halpern and deMause was a gradual process. Yet my own values showed through when I made certain decisions, while trying not to be offensive. One of my standards was to never invite someone a second time if they had failed to come the first time and were not at the point of death. Thus, when my friend Sid Halpern cancelled his meeting only weeks before it was to take place, he was never invited again despite my considerable affection and appreciation of him. In dealing with Lloyd deMause, for years I was conflicted about speaking freely. When Lloyd deMause hurt me by so abruptly terminating the Saturday workshops of the Institute for Psychohistory in 1982, I resolved that I would never allow him to have any significant control over my life in the future, but that I would continue to work with him to grow psychohistory. With Montague Ullman, there was no conflict because Monte was a master of helping individuals hear their own unconscious and conscious voices. This is the primary reason why I had such love and respect for him and cherish his memory.

In writing about the builders of psychohistory who are less well known than the six I have grouped in two chapters, I have mostly sought to give some understanding of their contributions and personalities as well as of my relationship to them. In conclusion, I would like to thank all of my colleagues, living and dead, for having created this wonderful field that I have had the pleasure of doing my part in building.

Notes

1 Some individuals enter analysis for the ideas generated, more than treatment, and they are like Woody Allen with psychoanalysts on the East and West Coasts. It should also be noted that far from all psychohistorians base their work on psychoanalysis.

2 David R. Beisel, *The Suicidal Embrace: Hitler, the Allies, and the Origins of the Second World War* (Nyack, New York: Circumstantial Productions, 2003).

3 Ian Kershaw, *Hitler 1889–1936 Hubris* (New York: W. W. Norton & Company, 2000).

4 To understand more about Lorenz' motivation, see Roger Lorenz, "Seventy Years of Exploring the Roots of Violence: A Personal Odyssey," *Clio's Psyche*, Vol. 2 No. 3 (December 1995): pp. 51–55.

5 Despite this and other frustrations, Ramapo College is both beautiful and a much better than average state liberal arts college.

6 When in our forties I chatted with my older brother regarding who was the favorite, it was interesting because we each thought the other was. At certain times and in certain ways, I think we were both correct about the other being favored.

7 I once taught the course, Winners and Losers in Presidential Politics, in Ramapo's now defunct Master of Liberal Studies Program.

APPENDICES

APPENDIX A

Featured Scholars, Editors, and Authors

Name	Institution	Interviewer	Publication Date
C. Fred Alford	U. Maryland	Paul H. Elovitz (PHE)	Mar. 2007
James W. Anderson	Northwestern	PHE	Winter 2018
David Bakan	York U.	Todd Dufresne	Sept. 1998
Herbert Barry	U. Pittsburgh	Bob Lentz (BL)/PHE	Sept. 2000
David Beisel	SUNY-RCC	BL	June 1994
Rudolph Binion	Brandeis U.	BL	Dec. 1994
Sue Erikson Bloland	Manhattan Institute	PHE	June 2005
Andrew Brink	U. Toronto	PHE	Sept. 1999
Donald Carveth	York U.	PHE	June 2006
^Molly Castelloe	*Clio's P.* Online Forum	BL	Mar. 2012
Marilyn Charles	Austen Riggs Center	PHE	2018
Nancy Chodorow	UC Berkeley	PHE/BL	Mar. 2005
Geoffrey Cocks	Albion College	PHE	Sept. 2004
Mary Coleman	Georgetown U.	PHE	Mar. 2001
Ralph Colp	Columbia	PHE	Sept. 2002
Lloyd deMause~	*J. Psychohistory*	BL	June 1996
Abram de Swaan	U. Amsterdam	Vivian Rosenberg	June 2001
John Demos	Yale U.	BL	June 1995
Daniel Dervin	Mary Washington U.	PHE	Sept. 2000
Alan Elms	UC Davis	Kate Isaacson	Dec. 2001
Paul H. Elovitz~	Ramapo College	Pauline Staines	June 1996
Paul H. Elovitz~	Ramapo College	Ken Fuchsman	June 2014
Paul H. Elovitz~	Ramapo College	Juhani Ihanus	Dec. 2015
Avner Falk	Hebrew U.	PHE	Dec. 1999
D. J. Fisher	*Int. J. Psychoanalysis*	PHE & Jacques Szaluta	Dec. 2015
John Forrester~	Cambridge U.	PHE	Sept. 2006

(*Continued*)

Name	Institution	Interviewer	Publication Date
Lawrence Friedman	Indiana U.	PHE/BL	Dec. 2003
Kenneth A. Fuchsman	U. Connecticut	PHE	Sp. 2017.
Betty Glad	U. South Carolina	PHE/BL	June 1999
Peter Gay	Yale U.	David Felix/PHE/BL	Sept. 1997
James Glass	U. Maryland	Fred Alford	June/Sept. 2007
Fred Greenstein	Princeton	PHE	June 2008
Carol Grosskurth	U. Toronto	BL	Sept. 1996
Carol Gilligan	NYU	PHE	Mar. 2004
Jay Y. Gonen	Veterans Admin.	PHE	Mar. 2001
Lynn Hunt	UCLA	BL	Mar. 1998
Norman Itzkowitz	Princeton	PHE	Dec. 2002
Sudhir Kakar	U. Hawaii/Harvard	PHE	Dec. 1998
Melvin Kalfus	Lynn U.	PHE	June 2000
Thomas Kohut	Williams	PHE/Geoffrey Cocks	Sept. 2005
George Kren	Kansas State U.	BL	Mar. 1995
Ken Fuchsman	U. Connecticut	PHE	Spring 2017
Henry Lawton	Psych. Film Group	PHE	Mar. 2003
Peter Loewenberg	UCLA	BL	Sept. 1994
David Lotto	*J. Psychohistory Editor*	PHE	Winter 2017
Robert Jay Lifton	Harvard	PHE	Dec. 1995
Elizabeth W. Marvick	UCLA	PHE/BL	June 2002
Bruce Mazlish	MIT	Tomasz Pawelec	Dec. 1996
Arthur Mitzman	U. Amsterdam	David Lee	Mar. 1999
Joseph Montville	George Mason U.	PHE	Dec. 2013
^Denis J. O'Keefe	IPA	PHE	Mar. 2013
Peter Petschauer	Appalachian State U.	Sally Atkins	June 1998
Philip Pomper	Wesleyan	PHE	June 2004
Daniel Rancour- Laferriere	UC Davis	PHE	June 2011
Carol Bird Ravenal	American U.	BL	Dec. 2011
Paul Roazen	York U.	BL	Mar. 1996
Stanley Renshon~	*Political Psychology*	BL	June 1996
Andrew Rolle	Occidental College	Cocks	Dec. 1997
William Runyan	UC Berkeley	Todd Schultz	Dec. 2001
Andrea Sabbadini ~	*Psychoanalysis & History*	PHE	Mar. 2001
Eli Sagan	Brandeis U.	PHE	June 2001
Joan Wallach Scott	Institute Advanced Study	PHE	Sept. 2014
Larry Shiner~	U. Illinois-Springfield	Mel Kalfus	June 1996
J. Lee Shneidman	Adelphi U.	PHE	June 2003
Dean Keith Simonton	UC Davis	Anna Song	Dec. 2001
Howard Stein	U. Oklahoma	Peter Petschauer	Mar. 2000
Charles B. Strozier	John Jay-CUNY	PHE	Mar. 1997
Strozier on Heinz Kohut	John Jay-CUNY	BL/PHE	Sept. 2001
Nancy Unger	Santa Clara U.	BL	Sept. 2011
George Vaillant	Harvard	PHE	Mar. 2007

Note: ^ indicates Young Scholar Interview

~ indicates Featured Editor Interview

APPENDIX B

Memorials in *Clio's Psyche*

Name and Life Dates	Author	Vol. No. Date	Page(s)
Rudolph Binion (1927–2011)★	Paul H. Elovitz	18, 2 Sept. 2011	200–209
	Deborah Hayden	18, 2 Sept. 2011	209–215
	Twenty-two colleagues	18, 2 Sept. 2011	215–238
Andrew Brink (1932–2011)	Paul H. Elovitz	18, 4 Mar. 2012	479–482
	Rachel Youdelman	18, 4 Mar. 2012	483–487
	George Johnson	18, 4 Mar. 2012	487–490
Sander Breiner (1925–2012)	Nancy Kobrin	19, 3 Dec. 2012	356–359
	Paul H. Elovitz	19, 3 Dec. 2012	359–360
Ben Brody (1920–2007)	Paul H. Elovitz	14, 3 Dec. 2007	101–102
L. Bryce Boyer (1926–2000)	Howard Stein	7, 3 Dec. 2000	162–164
Ben Brody (1920–2007)	Paul H. Elovitz David Felix	14, 3 Dec. 2007	101–102
Robert N. Butler [1927–2010]★	Nora O'Brien Suric Paul H. Elovitz	17, 3 Dec. 2010	266–269
Robert Chaikin (1947–1999)★	Paul H. Elovitz	6, 1 June 1999	40
Norman Cohn (1915–2007)	Henry R. Lawton	5, 1 June 2008	51–53
Ralph Colp (1924–2008)	Paul H. Elovitz et al.	15, 3 Dec. 2008	105, 160–163
Joseph Dowling (1926–2008)	Paul H. Elovitz	19, 3 Dec. 2012	355–356
Alan Dundes (1934–2005)	Howard F. Stein	12, 1 June 2005	33–34
Erik Erikson (1902–1994)	Leon Rappoport	1, 4 Mar. 1995	1–2
Lewis Feuer (1912–2002)	Paul H. Elovitz	9, 4 Mar. 2003	206–210
	Hans Bakker	9, 4 Mar. 2003	203–206
Bernard Flicker [1932–1995]★	David R. Beisel	2, 3 Dec. 1995	72
Michael Flynn (1962–2012)	Paul H. Elovitz	18, 3 Dec. 2012	360–361
John Forrester (1949–2015)	David Cifelli/PHE	23, 2, Winter 2017	214–216

(*Continued*)

Name and Life Dates	Author	Vol. No. Date	Page(s)
Peter Gay (1923–2015)	Ken Fuchsman	22, 1–2, June/Sept. 2015	115–119
William Gilmore (1945–1999)	Paul H. Elovitz	6, 1 June 1999	39–40
Betty Glad (1928–2010)	Nicole Alliegro/PHE	19, 2 Sept. 2012	240–241
Melvin Goldstein (1926–1997)	Paul H. Elovitz	4, 1 June 1997	32–33
Marvin Goldwert (1935–1995)	Paul H. Elovitz	2, 4 Mar. 1995	97
Charles Gouaux (1936–2006)	Paul H. Elovitz	13, 3 Dec. 2006	176
Sidney Halpern (1927–1994)	Baruch Halpern	2, 1 June 1995	6–8
H. Stuart Hughes (1916–1999)	Paul H. Elovitz	6, 3 June 1999	151
George M. Kren (1926–2000)	Paul H. Elovitz, et al.	7, 2 Sept. 2000	95–98
Mary Lambert (1920–2012)	Paul H. Elovitz	19, 2 Sept. 2012	239
Henry Lawton (1941–2014)	PHE/10 others	21, 1 June 2014	69–83
John E. Mack (1929–2004)	Paul H. Elovitz	12, 2 Sept. 2005	108–110
Elizabeth Marvick (1925–2005)	Betty Glad	12, 4 Mar. 2006	232–235
Bruce Mazlish (1923–2016)	Paul H. Elovitz	23, 3 Spring 2017	326–328
Alice Miller	Peggy McLaughlin	17, 3 Dec. 2010	260–263
Jean Baker Miller (1927–2006)	Teresa Bernadez	13, 3 Dec. 2006	173–176
Friedhelm Nyssen (1938–2003)	Peter Jüngst	11, 1 June 2004	25–27
Raphael Patai (1910–1996)	Paul H. Elovitz	3, 2 Sept. 1996	67
Otto Paul Pflanze (1919–2007)	Paul H. Elovitz	15, 2 Sept. 2008	101
Robert Pois (1940–2004)	Paul H. Elovitz	10, 4 Mar. 2004	161–162
Rita Ransohoff (1916–2003)	Joan Wynn Paul H. Elovitz	11, 1 June 2004	27–29
Leon Rappoport [1932–2009]★	Robert Downey	17, 3 Dec. 2010	264–266
Paul Roazen (1936–2005)	Daniel Burston	12, 3 Dec. 2005	165–166
	Donald Carveth	12, 3 Dec. 2005	166–167
Arnold A. Rogow (1924–2006)	Paul H. Elovitz Jeanne Rogow	13, 2 Sept. 2006	102–104
Eli Sagan (1927–2015)	Donald Carveth	22, 1–2, June/Sept. 2015	110–115
Richard L. Schoenwald [1927–95]★	Paul H. Elovitz	2, 3 Dec. 1995	72
Chaim Shatan (1924–2001)	Paul H. Elovitz	8, 2 Sept. 2001	102–103
Conalee Shneidman (1930–2007)	Paul H. Elovitz Peter Schwab	13, 4 Mar. 2007	224–226
Jerome Shneidman (1929–2008)	Paul H. Elovitz	15, 4 Mar. 2009	275–282
Mel Spiro (1920–2014)	David Cifelli/Joyce Rosenberg	23, 1 Fall 2016	87–88
Anthony Storr (1920–2001)	Andrew Brink	8, 2 Sept. 2001	93–97
Robert C. Tucker [1918–2010]★	Fred I. Greenstein	17, 3 Dec. 2010	257–259
Montague Ullman (1916–2008)	Judith Gardiner et al.	15, 2 Sept. 2008	57, 77–86
Robert G.L. Waite (1919–1999)	Thomas Kohut et al.	6, 3 June 1999	129–131
Eugene Victor Wolfenstein (1940–2010)	Paul H. Elovitz Bob Lentz	18, 2 Sept. 2011	238–241
Eugene Victor Wolfenstein	Peter Loewenberg	18, 2 Sept. 2011	242–245

Name and Life Dates	Author	Vol. No. Date	Page(s)
Elie Wiesel (1928–2016)	Eva Fogelman	23, 2, Winter 2017	216–221
Elizabeth Young-Bruehl (1946–2011)	Molly Castelloe/PHE	18, 4 Mar. 2012	490–496
Isaac Zieman (1920–2007)	Eva Fogelman /PHE	14, 1–2 June/Sept. 2007	33–36

*Square brackets indicate the life dates are not included in the title of the obituary.

INDEX

Made in the USA
Middletown, DE
08 February 2022